Aesthetic Intelligence
Reclaim the Power of Your Senses

Rochelle T. Mucha Ph.D.

Copyright © 2009 Rochelle T. Mucha Ph.D.
All rights reserved.

ISBN: 1-4392-3849-9
ISBN-13: 9781439238493

Visit www.booksurge.com to order additional copies.

PRAISE FOR
AESTHETIC INTELLIGENCE

Rochelle Mucha writes insightfully, generously and exceedingly well about a subject invisible to many, but nonetheless vital to our health as individuals and as a society, namely the centrality of our senses in learning, leadership, creativity and daily life. She introduces her very attractive concept of *Aesthetic Intelligence* with three rich underpinning capacities: *presence, authenticity and synthesis*, and then sets to work bringing each to life in refreshing, often profound, and ultimately elegant terms. "Listening", she says, "is not the work of one sense, but of all the senses." And it is listening at this deeper, more fully integrated level, which powers our capacity for *presence* and fuels Aesthetic Intelligence. She draws her concept of *authenticity* at a similar level of integration as a capacity which embraces the many roles we play in the course of a day or a lifetime with the same level of self-knowledge and steady fluency of being we witness in a first class actor. This too, fuels Aesthetic Intelligence. Whether you are a leader interested in sharpening your already keen sense of judgment, or an educator or consultant seeking new skills for the 21st century, Rochelle Mucha's book *Aesthetic Intelligence: Reclaim the Power of Your Senses* is bound to be an eye-opener, an ear opener, a mind opener and more. It will make you wonder why on earth you haven't come to your senses sooner!

    John J. Cimino, Jr.
    President & Founder, *Creative Leaps International* and
    The Learning Arts, composer, scientist, educational
    consultant, creator of the "Concert Of Ideas"

Aesthetic Intelligence is a journey that invites the reader to join Rochelle in being an organizational pioneer. Much like a playwright who invites actors to perform their work, Rochelle provides the stage for a new set of principles for managers, employees, or anyone in between, to take. It is up to you as the reader to explore your own Aesthetic Intelligence road. May you enjoy traveling the path as much as I have!
    William J. Latshaw, Organizational Practice Lead
    Researcher, Top Three Strategy Consulting Firm

The world has become a much less predictable place. Randomness has entered into world events like never before. The traditional management tools used to plan and predict for the future like MBO's and strategic planning models are becoming less effective. I found Ae© (Aesthetic Intelligence) to provide a fresh perspective that introduces new tools and concepts for dealing with the unpredictability leaders face today. The skills of presence, authenticity, and synthesis provide a new way to learn and adapt in this new reality. I loved the book and plan to share it with my team. Well done!
    Jim Burns, General Manager
    JW Marriott Orlando, Grande Lakes

I never knew there was so much to be learned about how to lead a business from such a disparate area as theatre. I found the book to be quite practical; and highlighted exactly what has been missing in business leadership. If you truly want to empower your organization for success, then this book is a must-read.
    Bobby Cooper
    Program Manager, The Coca-Cola Company

Rochelle brings a new and refreshing perspective to leadership. Her use of a theater arts metaphor highlights some of the most important leadership behaviors, giving Aesthetic Intelligence some real power.
    William Seidman, Ph.D.
    CEO, Cerebyte, Inc.

DEDICATION

To my granddaughters, Rayna and Aiden, for nurturing my creative spirit.

To my husband, Larry, for his enduring patience and loving encouragement.

CONTENTS

Prelude 1
The Aesthetic Intelligence Journey............................... 5
The Story of Aesthetic Intelligence 7
    Our Six Senses.. 7
    Ensemble Studies Reveal a Coveted Culture 9
    Peephole into the World of the Performing Arts........ 13
    In Contrast, a Typical Business Culture 19
    Business and the Arts Intersect 21
    Beyond Metaphor and Method: Aesthetic Intelligence
    Is Born.. 26
Aesthetic Intelligence... 29
    Basic Elements... 29
        Presence: Being and Acting in the Moment..................... 32
        Authenticity: Getting in Character with Intention........... 42
        Synthesis: Putting It Together.. 48
    Artistic Mindset: 'When' not 'What' 53
    Generative Conversation: Great Performances Require
    Great Connections! 57
Interlude…A Systems Perspective 67
    We Are Our Stories 69
    The Organization: Inside, Outside, and in the Middle 75
    Alignment: Design and Performance 79

Aesthetic Intelligence in Action 87
   Cultivating a Culture of Connection, Creativity,
   and Innovation 91
      Engagement: People Power 113
      The Language of Leadership 127
      Dramaturgy of Change 147
Not the Closing Curtain 157
Appendix One 161
   AeI© Self-Assessment 161
Appendix Two 173
   List of Interviewees 173
Appendix Three 175
   Recommended Resources 175
References 179
Index 185

PRELUDE

I am not a businessman. I am an artist.
Warren Buffett

When I was eight years old, my family went on a holiday to the Catskills Mountains. One of my cherished pictures taken there is one of my sister and me, clad in our Davy Crockett outfits, smiling with sheer joy. I never thought that fifty years after that picture was taken, I would be wearing my Davy Crockett outfit again. Okay, I admit I don't have the original outfit, and even if I did, it would not fit. But the image is symbolic and appropriate, because here I am today—a pioneer, exploring a new frontier. That may be where the comparison ends, as I do not see myself going down with something analagous to the Battle of the Alamo.

This book is about inviting you to be a pioneer too. Or, a wagon train follower, cautiously waiting for the pioneers to navigate a safe course. I will leave that choice to you.

Two years ago I completed my dissertation and, with that, my doctoral studies. I was a late bloomer, but I was determined to be ordained before I turned sixty. I think few people realize that a dissertation is simply a question that fetches a lot of time, uses up a lot of paper, and hopefully makes a contribution to a field of study. I entered my dissertation process with decades of experience working with leaders and organizations and was determined that my investment would be both fun and practical. I am a lover of the arts and had long been incorporating artistic methods in my work, be it in the boardroom or the classroom. This led me to set out and explore what business could learn from a theatre ensemble/company about alignment, the lack of which is a major thorn in the achilles heel of poor performance. I worked with two regional theatres in Atlanta, Georgia, and I had the time of my life.

I had planned on fully resuming my consulting activities when I finished my doctorate, but the universe had something else in mind. Clichés exist for a reason—they are universal, capture the human experience, and bear truth. My best laid plans never happened.

When I began my study, I thought I was a quirky management consultant born and raised in New York, home of Broadway, who fancied herself on imaginary stages. I never expected to stumble upon a discipline, an emergent field focused on Business and the Arts and, more specifically, Organizational Aesthetics. But I did. To my surprise there were artists, academics, and practitioners navigating new relationships between Business and the Arts. There was research—books, articles, and case studies—describing these emergent conversations. The playing field was comparatively small, and folks were primarily located outside of the United States. The majority of work revolved around the method and metaphors of the arts, but it was compelling. I was hooked!

When I finished my dissertation, I could not let go of the Pandora's Box that had been opened for me. I had to do something more to figure out a way to take what I had learned and make it useful to my clients and students. I wanted to go beyond metaphor and method.

That is what this book is about—the discovery and potential of *Aesthetic Intelligence* (AeI©).

I have organized this book by utilizing the same design principles that I use when creating a workshop or speech or when I am authoring a paper. I begin by getting us all on the same page and establishing a shared vocabulary. Understanding the journey and the culture of the performing arts is essential to appreciating the value of the intersection of Business and the Arts. From there, I introduce AeI© and its basic elements, *presence, authenticity* and *synthesis*, which when internalized enables us to reclaim the power of our senses and discover new ways of being, thinking, and doing. Before I begin illuminating applications, I spend some time discussing two key systems, both parallel and interdependent, the *self* and the *organization*. Throughout this discussion, I focus on how the critical alignment of these systems factor into overall performance. The final section is devoted to showing how to move from insight to practice. I begin with a discussion of familiar and resilient companies where AeI© is woven into the fabric of their organizations, resulting in cultures of connection, creativity, and innovation. I follow with discussions of engagement and leadership, two topics which are natural extensions of culture. I conclude this section with a conversation on how and why an Aesthetically Intelligent leader and an Aesthetically Intelligent organization are better prepared to flourish in times of relentless change and opportunity, since they will be able to move with certainty in uncertain environments. Following each of these chapters I offer ideas on what you might do differently within your sphere of influence, and I invite you to add your thoughts to the list. These ideas reflect and integrate the entire content of the book.

My objective in this final section is to demonstrate how AeI© and lessons learned from the world of the arts can inform organizational thinking and behavior, and play a role in how organizations can thrive in a global and innovative marketplace. Although I classify this book as a business text, and I reference leadership and employees, I believe the content is not limited by age, gender, or livelihood. Insights can serve business professionals and students, as well as inform our personal lives.

I want to be clear up front. I am not suggesting AeI© is the greatest thing since sliced bread or the only credible way of thinking. Nor am I suggesting that the elements of AeI© or the application ideas are unique in and of themselves. Quite the opposite. I think you will learn that by definition, AeI© demands an open mind, connection, and collaboration. It does not stand alone. It stands *with*. My goal is to expand your perspective and grow your

4 AESTHETIC INTELLIGENCE

toolbox—not empty it—to offer a novel way of approaching long-standing, widespread challenges and opportunities. I have intentionally kept this book brief, practical as opposed to scholarly, absent exhaustive amounts of data, case studies, and research. Rather, I would like to provoke your curiosity, spark your ideas, and encourage your continued exploration. I see this book as the beginning of a conversation that is full of possibilities, and I hope that by the time you are finished reading, your imagination and enthusiasm are soaring alongside my own.

Without any further delay, let's get started. Welcome to the AeI© journey.

THE AESTHETIC INTELLIGENCE JOURNEY...

Business and the arts are not different fields, but different aspects of the creative process.
Nancy Adler

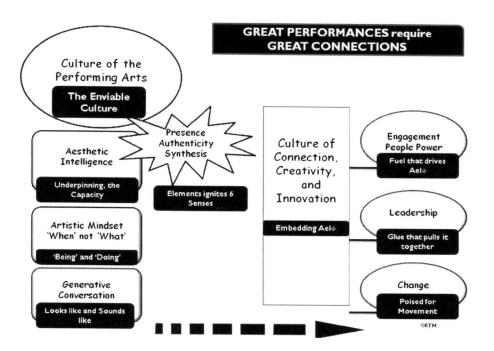

THE STORY OF AESTHETIC INTELLIGENCE

Imagination is more important than knowledge.
Albert Einstein

Our Six Senses

It is hard to resist children. Most of us are drawn to their infectious smiles and the way they play without abandon. Whether we are walking in a mall, supermarket, airport, or entering an elevator, our eyes will feast upon an infant or toddler perched atop his or her parent's shoulder. Chances are, you, like many others, have offered a smile to a resting infant and declared, "She is just so cute!" Sometimes the little one smiles back, causing the parent to say, "She likes you." Other times the little one turns her head away from you and retreats to the safety of her guardian.

My question is this: *How does that infant decide whether you are a person to smile for, or do the opposite - turn away and cry?* Babies do not read, write, or speak our language, so what factors inform their thinking, their responses, and their actions? I suggest little ones rely on their senses for this information and decide accordingly. Sensory knowing defines how we learn through our toddler years. Then slowly through socialization, we sadly and unknowingly relinquish the power of our senses to conform to traditional and narrower ways of knowing and being. The Technology and Knowledge Ages have shifted us into a virtual world, where our increasing dependency on the Internet, computers, and other devices has further dulled our senses. The good news is that we were all little once.

Reclaiming the power and potential of utilizing all our senses, the big five plus one—intuition—is the essence of AeI©. Our minds have been programmed to associate the term "aesthetic" with beauty, but the root of the word aesthetic refers to the employment of our senses. To be *Aesthetically Intelligent* is to fully engage our senses—to see, hear, touch, smell, taste, and intuit—in all our interactions. And when we do this, we release ourselves from the shackles of mindless experiences and, consequently, constrained decision-making, problem solving, and creativity.

Why use one or two senses when we have six? Educator and author Virginia Griffin asks, "Would a musician play a one-string guitar"[1]? Of course not! You don't have to be a guitarist to know that a musician would not opt for a one-string guitar in lieu of the standard six-string instrument. The magic in making and listening to music comes from the rich harmony of notes and chords. Musicians mix and mingle guitar strings to create a range of rhythms and melodies. Fewer strings would compromise the music and render the guitar barren. The six strings of a guitar parallel our six senses and beg the following questions: Why do humans often opt to utilize one sense when we have six? Why just hear, when we can see, smell, taste, touch, and, of course, intuit? Why settle on being rational when we can embrace what is relational, emotional, social, and physical?

We understand the world through our senses, and it is through our senses that we perceive. Each day offers an abundance of perceptions that ignite a tapestry of sensual responses. Imagine the richness of experience that awaits you if you consciously employ the senses available to you, transforming daily experiences into meaningful knowing, being, and doing. Pine and Gilmore[2] authors of *The Experience Economy*, concur that "the more sensory an experience, the more memorable it will be". They go on to say that creating this sensory experience should be intentional, not ad hoc.

The elements of Aesthetic Intelligence, presence, authenticity, and synthesis, depend on such use of our senses. Learning about

AeI© will illuminate how we can reclaim the power of our senses, enhance our capabilities, and, in turn, enhance how we can better serve our organizations. But before we go there, I would like to tell you how I came to know of AeI©.

Ensemble Studies Reveal a Coveted Culture

My dissertation study proved to be one of the most memorable journeys of my life. As stated, my intention was rather simple. I wanted to explore what business organizations could learn from theatre ensembles to enhance alignment and performance. Beyond completing dissertation requirements, I hoped to discover insights that would strengthen my ability as a management consultant to work with and support my clients. That was my stated professional goal.

Choosing to work with theatre was easy for me. As long as I could remember, I approached my work as theatre. I would "audition" for prospects, hoping they would become clients. I would identify "roles," and then "cast" my team. I would create a working "script," align folks in front of and "behind the scenes," and strive to delight the "house." I suspect this bias stems from my alter ego, the Broadway performer who never made it past school plays and singing in the shower.

I could hardly contain my personal excitement as I began to work with theatre ensembles. I was like a kid in a candy store. I soaked in every observation, from audition to opening night. I interviewed over forty-five actors and technical staff, onstage and backstage. The experience was more than I ever imagined. I share excerpts from some those interviews throughout this book and provide a partial list of interviewees in the appendix. Complete interview transcripts are published within my dissertation [3].

Aside from personal curiosity, looking at theatre for lessons on the relationship between people, passion, and performance made sense to me. After all, most everyone has attended theatre. Theatre is a microcosm of life, and the experience is universal. Audiences worldwide listen attentively, move to the rhythm of words and/or music, and eagerly recognize the talent at the final curtain. Theatre engages people!

Consider that on July 25, 1975, *A Chorus Line* opened on Broadway and closed there on April 28, 1990, after 6,137 performances. For some time, it held the record as the longest-running musical in history. While all shows are a result of collaboration, *A Chorus Line* particularly owed its success to its creator, Michael Bennett. Never had a director and choreographer been so dominant in a show's formation. Bennett wanted a show that spotlighted "gypsies," a theatrical term for chorus dancers. He wanted to honor a dancer's life. Yet he also knew that the musical had to have commercial audience appeal.

A Chorus Line proved to be the optimal blending of all its performance elements, and it revolutionized the way audiences viewed musical theatre. It broke away from the rigid story line of traditional musicals, intertwining the stories of the ensemble cast into a seamless whole. In the words of reviewer Frank Rich, "It was the stitching together of all its elements in that purest of theatrical areas, a deep and empty stage by its director-choreographer that made *A Chorus Line* so thrilling to its audience" [4].

A Chorus Line won many awards. In 1975 it received the New York Drama Critics Circle Award, the Pulitzer Prize for Drama, CLIO Finalist Certificate, and the Hollywood Radio & Television Society International Broadcasting Award; in 1976 it received nine Tony Awards, five Drama Desk Awards, the Los Angeles Drama Critics Circle Award, Special Theatre World Reward, the Obie Award; in 1977 it received the London Evening Standard Award; in 1978 a Gold Record Award from Columbia Records, and in 1984, it won a special Tony as the Longest Running Show in Broadway history [5].

A Chorus Line remains an enviable combination of artistic achievement and popular appeal. It may not represent all musical theatre productions, but it certainly goes down in history as a production that enjoyed and continues to enjoy success back on Broadway today. People in and out of the theatre found their own stories on that stage—joys, disappointments, fears, memories, and hopes. It was a masterful production of seamless integration that created a consistent singular sensation every day and every night for fifteen years. I thought surely, there must be something the world of business can learn from such a huge success. This assumption guided my study.

I worked with two fabulous artistic directors, Mira Hirsch of the Jewish Theatre of the South, and Susan Booth of the Alliance Theatre, recipient of the 2007 Tony award for best regional theatre. Through their generosity, I came to understand and appreciate the world of the performing arts.

My inquiry stemmed from over twenty years as an organizational consultant, internal and external. I have witnessed how organizational performance is compromised by misalignments (gaps between rhetoric and action, process and behavior). The greater the number and scope of misalignments, the more results are compromised. Even seemingly small misalignments erode performance and, unfortunately, often remain unnoticed by organizational leaders. I thought about *A Chorus Line* and its consistent, long-term success. I wondered how it all came together, and more importantly, how this type of performance is sustained.

This musing led me in search of the Holy Grail, the magical underpinning of theatre that would remedy the rampant misalignment in business organizations. I did not find it. What I did discover was that the world of performing arts, and in my case specifically theatre, embodied a well-oiled machine with a deeply embedded culture that would be the envy of any business organization I know. I discovered a place where:

- Team play is a given, and everyone has their eye on the same prize;
- Feedback is daily and embedded;

- Experimentation informs structure, is welcomed and not punished;

- Individuals passionately and proudly invest 100 percent of their energy and focus every day;

- Pride and playfulness, compromise and competency, self-interest and collaboration, and structure and freedom stand side by side.

What's more, I found that these enviable attributes were implicit, not promoted with team buildings, pep rallies, town halls, road shows, mission statement plaques, and laminated cards.

These coveted cultural attributes describe the culture of the performing arts: a world where ego, self-direction, and individuality aptly describe the players; respect, connection, and dependency describe how they play. Such a place was not imaginary. Such a place captured the aspirational rhetoric exuded about culture in the business world. But it was not rhetoric; it was reality in the world of the performing arts.

Like any organization, an ensemble is a system, a group of interdependent elements forming a complex whole; an ensemble is a condition of harmonious interaction. It is a dynamic integration of performers, which taps the inherent energy and skills of members and demands that each individual is aware of how his or her work aligns with fellow actors. Performance is the culmination of their shared efforts. This description is in keeping with authors Rob Austin and Lee Devin, who in their text *Artful Making*, define an ensemble as "a working group whose product is greater than the sum of its parts" [6]. I came to believe that whenever companies integrate the outcomes of work across disparate business performances, they too perform theatre.

One actor I interviewed for my study described the ideal audience experience as one when the patron feels like he or she "is peeping through a keyhole, observing real life in action." With that in mind, I invite you take a peep at this coveted culture. As you read the following half dozen pages, I encourage your curiosity and reflection. It may seem unnecessary to offer this detailed a picture of the typical culture of the performing arts; however, appreciating this culture is necessary for acknowledging and respecting the differences between it and the typical culture of the world of business. This distinction underlies the content of this book and subsequently optimizes your learning. As you read, I also ask you to bear in mind that I am describing my experience and understanding of the core and timeless values of the performing arts. In no way am I suggesting that all ensembles are perfect, but I am suggesting that these foundational values are typical and reveal insights for business leaders.

Peephole into the World of the Performing Arts

The appearance of theatre dates back to the beginning of humankind, to the onset of civilization. It seems theatre, a form of storytelling, is an innate human need. The culture of the theatre today has changed little from its roots. Historically, even before the time of the Renaissance, theatre was socially and physically in a class by itself. Erected on the margins of the mainstream, theatrical cities came to be known as "spectacular" societies. Theatre districts were frequently a cultural haven; they were often experimental and sometimes socially or morally banished. Then, like today, theatre appeared to occupy a free space outside the reach of authorities, a place between two worlds.

The secular nature of the arts was related with stories shared by Alan Alda in his memoir *Never Have Your Dog Stuffed* [7]. Robert Alda, his father, ran a burlesque house, and Alan spent many a childhood day there, viewing his father from backstage. Alda tells readers that it was during that time that he realized there was one life behind the floodlights, and there was another life off stage, on the other side of the lights. An actor needs to be able to live completely in both worlds. My research immersed me in the worlds of artists who live on both sides of the floodlights. I want to emphasize to my reader what was often emphasized to me: I am speaking about *professional* theatre, not community theatre. The people I interviewed and observed were *professionals*, not people pursuing a hobby. Here is a glimpse of my experiences gleaned from interviews and observations.

Learning about the culture of theatre took prodding. I received blank stares when I asked ensemble members to describe their culture. It was clearly implicit, not explicit. Folks usually began by telling me how they perceived others labeled theatre professionals: liberal, weird, different, nonconforming. The people with whom I spoke universally thought that the average person or patron did not understand theatre as a culture and an industry. Yet I discovered it was the culture and its uniqueness that drew residents in and kept them there. Chris, a lighting designer, shares:

> Once you get bit by the acting bug, that's it. That is what you want to do forever. This is an addictive business. You cannot leave. Everyone goes through periods of time when they think they would want to work nine to five. I bet 90 percent have tried and failed at it. [Theatre] is like quicksand, a love-hate quicksand. It does not let go of you. I only know one person who left the business, for health reasons. No one leaves the theatre.

A few seasoned professionals whimsically spoke of wishing they could do something else or go somewhere else, lamenting their *fate*. These words were capricious. The notion of not being in theatre evoked visible and articulated fear. Sarah, director, captured an artist's reality, a characteristic cultural elation, when she said, "I love the fact that I live a lifestyle that is an artistic one [different from a typical business lifestyle and environment]." The unconventional quality of theatre attracts and keeps its players.

Some cultural aspects I learned were not surprising. I expected theatre to be outside the norm. I expected to hear about collaboration and compromise. But I was stunned when I realized what a significant role competency and time play in defining theatre culture. This was a revelation.

Competency enfolds in two ways. First, it guides individuals as they strive to achieve personal mastery and earn respect from their peers. This is why the first script read through on the first day of rehearsal is so daunting. Each person wants to leave feeling the other cast members are confident in his or her ability to play the role. Isaac, actor, verbalized this emotion, saying, "Everybody has the same need to show that you really belong. If there is going to be a weak link, it is not going to be me." This insight explains how the need for individual competency is a driving factor toward alignment and interdependency. Such individuals do not want to disappoint the whole group.

The second way competency rears its head in theatre is as a driver of compromise and collaboration. Actors want a director to give them space, to allow them to feel out their character and play with the role. At the same time, actors want to partner with a director. TECH staff members want a director to respect their expertise and work within given constraints. Both actors and TECH staffers want to have a voice. Both expect the director to make final decisions and will follow directions even if they feel they were not as respected or engaged as they wanted. They do this if they deem the person giving the orders, be it on stage or behind the scenes, as competent. In the initial phases of my research, I hypothesized cast and crew willingly and happily surrendered self for others. Learning the importance of competency and how it influences collaboration dismantled my naiveté. Feelings about compromise and collaboration are intimately laced with individual evaluations of competency.

Theatre is a paradoxical culture of self-interest and collaboration. Those who join are clearly self-directed and seek individual success, even fame. Yet at the same time, they recognize that without the ensemble, an individual does not exist; without an audience, theatre does not exist. Only together can one's self-interest be actualized. Interdependency is a central value of theatre.

Pride in self, work product, and company performance is a strong value of theatre culture. Theatre professionals are builders of characters, scenes, stories, and sets. This brand of pride fosters Esprit de Corps, the commitment from ensemble members to deliver the playwright's message, which nurtures an individual and shared sense of accomplishment. Pride is evidenced by enthusiastic devotion to members of a group and its purpose. Pride helps explain why people are driven to work their hardest even when they are unhappy with an individual or an individual decision. Even when grappling with disappointments or the nagging presence of a diva, theatre professionals do not compromise their performance. Their name, their credibility, and thus, their pride are on the playbill.

By definition, the culture of theatre is one of acceleration. There are a mere few weeks to go from nothing to opening night. It is an amazing process. The ensemble, which can be likened to a business task force, has little time to move through stages of team development. Relationships form quickly. Time constraints are non-negotiable. Time does not permit teambuilding; team play is a given. Limited time demands trust be given blindly, and this plays out very differently from typical business relationships, where a great deal of time is often spent attempting to earn trust.

Theatre is a messenger of ideas, a facilitator of learning, and an impetus for discussion. Theatre offers a one-time experience that creates lingering memories. Unlike its contemporary counterparts such as film and television, which viewers can easily see multiple times, a theatre production is never exactly the same twice. Theatre is provocative. Good theatre holds a mirror up to life for humanity to look into and to better understand itself. The notion theatre exists to inform and change lives was echoed frequently by its residents. Christopher, an actor, described theatre as a safe "forum for the big ideas." Joe thought it "important for human beings to watch themselves." BJ, a director, strived to "find the most potent and powerful ways to challenge [the audience] to think, to feel, and to revisit their beliefs." From their view, art is a medium of social construction.

The players regard theatre as a tool, a vehicle to help others learn about being human. They bring life to what otherwise would remain the sole propriety of a playwright. Richard Dreyfuss, film and theatre actor, concurs with the professional actors I met when he shares the following.

> People say, "Well you actors you just say these words. They're not yours." That's true but the genius of Shakespeare could not be felt or understood without the actor saying those words. And no matter how much you read them on the page the acting is going to make them into something else. And that is a noble calling. An actor never says to himself "these are mine. I wrote them." He knows that he is the mechanism - the Rube Goldberg device - the thing that is the connective tissue between understanding and appreciation and that genius. There's a huge visceral pleasure, sensual pleasure out of that experience. [8]

Susan Booth says, "Theatre captures and celebrates human practice … theatre is about being human, to elicit the emotions of the audience." She likens this process to the ritual in Greek Society when members of society would gather four times a year to watch theatre. Plays were designed to engage the audience to discuss and resolve common concerns. Probing the culture of theatre provided a stunning example of shared mission. Everyone involved in theatre shared a common goal, to tell a writer's story.

Theatre is a culture of experimentation, a culture that inherently assumes trial and error, failure and recovery. I watched actors try out different ways to embody their characters and move in different directions to engage with other actors on stage. These experiments may or may not be discussed in advance but were always discussed afterwards. It is part of the collaborative discipline. The actors cannot know exactly how any action will play out until they are together. Storytelling requires multiple hands.

No one was ever encouraged *not* to experiment. No one was ever ridiculed or chastised when their experiments did not work. They did, however, often laugh at themselves. The culture of experimentation renders theatre more likely to relinquish the obsolete and less likely to fall prey to inertia. Quite the opposite regularly occurs in business environments.

Rehearsals are a time and place to experiment, hosting different ways (runs) to perform the play - stumble through the script (proceed without stopping no matter what), work through (stop the action at anytime to discuss, and modify) and design runs (includes cast and props). Celebrated actor Ellen Burstyn shares, "For me it's all about rehearsal. The more time you have rehearsing and exploring and delving into a character, the deeper the work is. Deep exploration takes repetition and time" [8]. Given the brevity of time, rehearsal is intense.

Through my experiences, I began to understand how actors embrace their roles. The role, the character, is like a suit of clothes across the room, and it is the actors' job, their obligation, to walk across the room and get into that suit of clothes. Rehearsals provide the space, physically and emotionally, to explore, test, and gel the movements, sounds, and postures, which will communicate the writer's story. All this is accomplished in a discrete, non-negotiable span of time. Rehearsal is a key process of becoming authentic; it is a time of intentional characterization.

Structures, protocols, and process are clear and followed but not explicitly stated. There are no instructions, no guidebook. Tenured and novice participants implicitly know the rules of the road, how things are done. Structure and freedom coexist. This presents somewhat of a paradox since conforming to the rules is not a cultural attribute in theatre. I found that adherence to protocol was another indicator of the power of cultural norms, as opposed to formal rules that control individual behavior.

There is no lack of candor in theatre; it is a culture of criticism. However, there are clear channels on how candor and feedback are shared. Actors do not tell other actors what to do differently. They do not critique performances. Only the director shares feedback through written or verbal notes and one-on-one conversations. The producer does not share comments regarding production or performance issues with the individuals but speaks through the director. This protocol avoids confusion and ensures cast and crew do not receive mixed messages. The buck stops with the director.

The culture of theatre is a place where trust is given before it is earned. Mistakes are expected, not punished. Players abide by a host of unwritten protocols. Feedback is ongoing. Affection is visible and audible. Uncertainty is certain. Fun is promoted. People are proud and open-minded. Struggles with time and money constraints are the norm. These are the values of theatre, the basic beliefs and assumptions, which dictate behavior.

In Contrast, a Typical Business Culture

In my experience, there are several striking differences between the culture of theatre and the typical business environment. I admit in advance the following comments are generalizations, but I feel they can serve as a vehicle for making distinctions and drawing parallels between the arts and business. You may resonate with some, none, or all of the organizational ailments I cite. To be clear, these generalizations are not condemnations of business—quite the contrary. I have great respect, admiration, and even affection for my business clients and students, and like many others in my field, I am constantly seeking ways to help organizations achieve and sustain the productive work culture and environment for which they strive. This book is one attempt. One final caveat – when I speak of a "typical" business culture, I am referring to the evolved, mature business environment as opposed to the "garage or attic" conception stage that gave rise to such entities as Dell and Facebook.

In the business world, I have found culture commonly discussed and referred to as a screening factor—who is in and who is out or who fits and who does not fit. Culture is used to label an environment, justify behavior, sometimes supportive and sometimes coercive with its members. Contrary to my interactions with theatre professionals, employees frequently feel more stuck than lucky.

There is a wide range of business cultures, from passive to aggressive, from defensive to constructive. Business cultures appear comparatively unstable, an environment where internal and external culture change agents are commonplace. Business culture is fair game, vulnerable to change caused by new leadership and technology or a merger/acquisition. Business entities seem to favor revolution, while the arts prefer evolution.

Candor is often a culprit in business cultures. There is usually too much or too little candor, which frequently results in miscommunication, muddled expectations, and disappointing performances. Instead of confronting each other with direct feedback, individuals in a business environment often talk and complain about each other through sidebar and third-party conversation. Trust is earned in droplets and lost in bucketfuls. Certainty is more comfortable and valued than uncertainty. Physical affection is frowned upon, and in most cases, limited by labor laws. Human emotion is guarded.

There is never enough time in business, yet time is continually wasted on perceived useless meetings and layers of decision-making. There is an abundance of protocols and dictated systems, many of which outlive their usefulness, hindering rather than helping people and the organization become successful.

Competency is equated with results, but both can take a backseat to organizational politics and just plain luck. The corporate landscape is cluttered with competent individuals who rose to great heights at the cost, rather than the benefit, of their organization. Related to competency is the term *talent*, and the process talent management, terms heavy with rhetoric and light with action. Collaboration and shared visions are rallied and documented ad nauseaum. Mistakes are avoided for fear of looking foolish and/or suffering recrimination. Pride is a word on a plaque, and rarely an articulated emotion that drives behavior. Too often employees are in it for themselves, not the company, or the associated product or service.

Most employees know little about their actual external or end customer and product, and would be hard pressed to tell you what difference their organization is making in the world, yet alone what difference they are making as an individual. This can translate into an absence of purpose and meaningfulness.

Given the coveted attributes of the culture of the performing arts, business learning from the artist's world should be a no brainer. Unfortunately, the glaring contrast between the two worlds often poses barriers rather than connections. This is a lost opportunity. After all, the success of an organization, no matter its mission, no matter if it is for profit or if it is a nonprofit, depends on the culture and cohesive energy of its people. Culture is omnipotent in whatever entity it prevails: an organization, community, or a country. Culture is not something an organization has; culture is something an organization is, a social energy that moves people to act. Culture is not just another piece of the puzzle; it is the puzzle. Given the enviable qualities of the culture of the performing arts and the current and ongoing market challenges and opportunities business is confronting, I daresay, business cannot afford to ignore the world of the performing arts. Indeed, I propose the elements that have come together to capture the hearts and minds of audiences for centuries in the performing arts are the same elements that can come together in the future to result in businesses that are built to last.

Business and the Arts Intersect

There are two critical and ongoing imperatives for business today that transcend daily news headlines.

- To cultivate an environment of connection and creativity, leading to innovation.
- To develop robust and healthy relationships in a diverse and global marketplace.

Both of these demand a cultural environment that the majority of businesses have failed to create, a culture characterized by the very attributes that define the world of performing arts. A place where players on stage and behind the scenes share a common goal, are passionate and energetic, play well with others, are not just open to new thoughts but seek them out, give and receive feedback often, experiment without fear, and take pride in their interdependency.

It is not surprising then to learn that many organizations and business schools have turned to the arts for help. Around the world, centers for excellence have surfaced in Canada, England, and Denmark. AACORN (Arts, Aesthetics, Creativity and Organization Research Network) is an informal global membership of artists, academics, and practitioners exploring the intersections between business and the arts. These founding mothers and fathers are pioneers in the emergent field of organizational aesthetics.

Artistic metaphors and methods have been employed to dramatize business culture, instigate imagination, and enhance teamwork and customer experiences. Role characterizations illuminate parallels between a typical director and a business leader. The arts have long been a source to teach presentation and media skills. Poetry by David Whyte inspired business leaders and has become a frequent method of teaching leadership for Ronald Heifetz, director of the Leadership Education Project at Harvard University [9]. Music ensembles and orchestras facilitate learning about leadership and teams. This is evidenced by the work of John Cimino, of Creative Leaps International, and also captured by Ben Zander, Conductor of the Boston Philharmonic, in his text *Leadership: An Art of Possibility*[10], which has been translated into seventeen languages. The Academy of Management, an icon of business academia and the publication, Organization Science, partnered to devote an entire journal edition to illuminating how jazz and improvisation can be used to foster creativity and innovation [11]. A partial bibliography revealing the depth and breadth of the intersection of business and the arts is available to you in the appendix.

The relationship of business and the arts has begun to permeate trade literature. The September 2007 edition of *Fast Company* highlighted how "design" is taking on new meaning and power in the world economy. Chris Hacker, Chief Design Officer of Johnson & Johnson, explains why he hired designer Yves Behar, founder of the FuseProject: "I hired Yves because he's a game changer ... he has the ability to strip something down to its basic functional logic and then apply a set of emotional and aesthetic considerations to create something unique. It's an art" [12]. Virginia Postrel, author and speaker, explains why she advocates an aesthetic imperative:

> When we decide how next to spend our time or money, considering what we already have and the costs and benefits of various alternatives, "look and feel" is likely to top our list. We don't want more food, or even more restaurant meals—we're already maxed out. Instead, we want tastier, more interesting food in an appealing environment. It's a move from physical quantity to intangible, emotional quality [13].

The term *aesthetic* used in these examples is in keeping with the definition I have offered and refers to creating a complete experience that captures the engagement of our senses. These design leaders have helped their customers understand and value the complementary nature of design and experience.

Business leaders are espousing new vocabulary. Warren Buffet claims, "I am not a businessman; I am an artist." Robert Lutz, former General Motors Product Chief, reflects, "I see us being in the art business. Art, entertainment and mobile sculpture, which, coincidentally, also happens to provide transportation [14]". Mark Parker started his career as a designer for Nike, and now, as CEO, he ensures that design always has a strong voice in determining strategy. These voices are joined by other business leaders

(P &G, Unilever, Cisco, Intel, IBM, Hewlett-Packard, and more) who are turning to the world of the arts for insight and guidance [15].

Several studies strengthen the growing intersection of business and the arts. A 2008 Conference Board study reports that employers agree the "ability to identify new patterns of behavior or new combination of actions and integration of knowledge across different disciplines are foremost in demonstrating creativity, and that arts training is crucial to developing creativity" [16]. The 2008 Upwardly Global MBA, a survey of more than one hundred executives spread across twenty countries and published by *Harvard Business Review*, claimed that leaders wanted "recruits who were more thoughtful, more aware, more sensitive, more flexible—in short, people with the soft skills to effectively act upon the knowledge they have" [17]. In December 2008, the Task Force on the Arts at Harvard University advocated sweeping changes to foster the intersection of the arts across disciplines. The report concluded:

> Students are entering a new and rapidly changing economy, one in which fertile imagination, inventiveness, the control of recalcitrant materials, improvisational cunning, empathy, and the ability at once to master and to violate conventions will be at least as important as the bodies of knowledge they will acquire in their classes. They grasp that they will be called upon, in almost anything they eventually do, to show a capacity for collaborative creativity. They want to learn how to wed passionate energy to a sense of balance, proportion, grace, and fitness. [18]

Unfortunately, business schools are ill-equipped to cater to these evolving business needs. Rakesh Khurana, author of *From Higher Aims to Hired Hands* and professor at Harvard Business School, critiques the typical B-School. He claims they no longer are focused on producing far-sighted leaders who can help the economy run better; rather, they are engaged in a race to steer students to high-paying finance and consulting jobs, without caring about the graduates' broader roles in society [19]. Abraham Zaleznik, Professor of Leadership Emeritus at Harvard University, concurs:

> It seems to me that business leaders have much more in common with artists, scientists, and other creative thinkers than they do with managers. For business schools to exploit this commonality of dispositions and interests, the curriculum should worry less about the logics of strategy and imposing the constraints of computer exercises and more about thought experiments in the play of creativity and imagination. If they are successful, they would then do a better job of preparing exceptional men and women for positions of leadership. [20]

My experience serving as adjunct faculty also bears witness to the overwhelming influence of the AASCB (Association to Advance Collegiate Schools of Business) standards on curriculum, which suffocate business school offerings. I am shocked and dismayed at how little my students know about organizational culture, leadership, engagement, and change.

The growing intersection of business and the arts have left B-schools scrambling to make appropriate curriculum changes. Daniel Pink, author of *A Whole New Mind,* championed such change, concluding that "we're progressing yet again to a society of creators and empathizers, of pattern recognizers and meaning makers" [14]. Pink asserts the new MBA is the MFA (Master of Fine Arts), a degree of increasing popularity. He supports his claim by reporting that this trend is evidenced by the fact that McKinsey Consulting, long touted as the single largest employer of MBA (Master of Business Administration) graduates, has reduced the number of MBA grads they hire by nearly 20 percent in the last decade as they seek out more well-rounded candidates.

Further pressure stems from publications such as the annual *Wall Street Journal* survey of MBA schools. In September 2007, they reported that without exception, the B-schools that increased their rank did so because of increased focus on holistic and experiential activities coupled with fostering teamwork and collaboration. Arts-based learning is breaking disciplinary boundaries and has become a staple in such universities as Babson, Wharton, UCLA, Columbia, McGill, Copenhagen, and Essex. New York University broke new ground in Fall 2007 by offering the first dual MBA/MFA, a partnership among their Tisch School of the Arts, Kanbar Institute of Film and Television and the Stern School of Business. Stanford University opened the Hasso Plattner Institute of Design in Fall 2008. This school was inspired by David Kelley, founder of IDEO, and does not grant any terminal degrees. Instead, it offers specialized graduate programs focused on cultivating *creative confidence*, individual creativity and competency. Stanford is now considering offering *creative confidence* as a graduation requirement similar to that of a foreign language. Emory University in Atlanta, Georgia has established a Center for Creativity and Arts, inspired by Stanford's endeavor.

These examples demonstrate the increasing comingling of business and the arts. However, these approaches have serious limitations. Much of the work to date has focused on a specific artistic method or metaphor (jazz, poetry, improvisation), which are often event-driven, onetime special sessions. This piecemeal approach, similar to taking a team out to rock climb or brave the rapids, shortchanges each party and often delivers short-lived returns. Failure to integrate insights and skills from the arts into the fabric of organizational life endangers its value to being reduced to a fad, a trend, or a flavor of the month. I believe it is both an imperative and an opportunity to look beyond method and metaphor.

Beyond Metaphor and Method: Aesthetic Intelligence Is Born

Although terribly enthused about the potential of what the arts could offer business and business leaders, my research made me recognize how daunting, if not impossible, it was to transplant cultures. *Was there an underlying capacity of the culture of the performing arts? Could the underpinning be identified? Could this be taught?*

The answer became evident while I was working on a paper for the Art of Management Conference [21]. My collaborator, Constance Goodwin, Ph.D., was a former performing artist who created a thriving career as a leadership consultant and coach. Our paths crossed, and we agreed to author a paper. Our collaboration was exhilarating, our weekly dialogue expansive. Each of us brought our experience to uncharted territory. It was during these lively exchanges that AeI© was born.

When we probed deeper beyond the superficial methods and metaphors of the artist's world, we discovered the capacities that defined its culture and behavior. Deep listening. Intentional characterization. The ability to synthesize experience and data and act in real time. These foundational skills and behaviors encompass the basic elements of the expansive capacity, AeI©, which are intricately dependent on the utilization of all our senses. AeI© defines the *Artistic Mindset.*

More importantly, these were the precise skills and behaviors required to address the universal challenges of cultivating an environment of connection, creativity, and innovation, and developing robust and healthy relationships in a diverse and global marketplace. Internalizing AeI© could help remedy our atrophied *sense* ability and encourage new forms of cognitive behavior to extend our intellectual and creative reach beyond traditional boundaries. Learning and embedding these capacities could indeed transform a culture and enable business organizations to better tackle their challenges and opportunities.

I want to make a critical distinction that is important to understand before reading any further. There is ample evidence of the use of the arts as a metaphor for business. I am not suggesting AeI© as a metaphor or saying that business actors should mimic what artists do. Rather I am offering a richer insight, an opportunity to learn from what sources artists act, what they bring as they stare at a blank canvas or turn the first page of a new script. AeI© is a capacity, a way of being, which, in turn, informs desired ways of doing.

During an interview with Business Radio Atlanta, Jeff Davis asked me, "What could business learn from theatre? I thought it was the other way around and that theatre has a lot to learn from business." My reply then and now is the same. The relationship between business and the arts is a mutual relationship. There is no doubt that the typical world of theatre is different from the typical business enterprise, but different does not equate to right or wrong, good or bad. The relationship between the arts and business can be egalitarian, not adversarial. To achieve and sustain success, each must master the creative process of performance and relationship. Each world has much to learn from each other. Each world shares an imperative to create a culture where engagement, creativity, and innovation flourish. This book's focus is on what business can learn from the performing arts.

AeI© introduces a fresh way to think about how to optimize our individual and organizational performance. The next section describes the interdependent elements of AeI©, which compose the essence of an artistic mindset and render *Generative Conversation* possible.

AESTHETIC INTELLIGENCE

If art is the bridge between what you see in your mind and what the world sees, the skill is how you build that bridge.
Twyla Tharp

Basic Elements

We have come a long way from the simplicity of the Intelligence Quotient, the IQ, infamous discriminator between the haves and have nots. Howard Gardner is perhaps best known for shattering the intelligence myth in his groundbreaking text *Frames of Minds: The Theory of Multiple Intelligences*, now in its tenth edition.

> In the heyday of the psychometric and behaviorist eras, it was generally believed that intelligence was a single entity that was inherited; and that human beings—initially a blank slate—could be trained to learn anything, provided that it was presented in an appropriate way. Nowadays an increasing number of researchers believe precisely the opposite; that there exists a multitude of intelligences, quite independent of each other; that each intelligence has its own strengths and constraints; that the mind is far from unencumbered at birth; and that it is unexpectedly difficult to teach things that go against early "naïve" theories that challenge the natural lines of force within an intelligence and its matching domains. [22]

Gardner's goal then and over time was not to assign merit rankings to the range of intelligences identified but rather to encourage educators and individuals to discover their various aptitudes. He believed this self-knowledge would facilitate the synthesis of understanding ourselves and that this, in turn, would improve and expand our capability.

Gardner's work set the stage for Daniel Goleman, who would find success with *Emotional Intelligence* [23]. Goleman did not invent the notion of self-awareness, but he did package it in such a way so that it made sense to individuals across a vast landscape. Through research and practice, he substantiated that if one were *self-aware*, then he or she would be more likely to *self-manage*, possess strong *empathy* skills, and subsequently enjoy robust *social* relationships. These four attributes defined Emotional Intelligence, and Goleman established a positive correlation between a high EQ (Emotional Quotient) and stellar leadership. It appears that the role of IQ pales in comparison to EQ, accounting for less than 10 percent of career success. A high IQ may get you the job, but a high EQ would get you promoted.

While Goleman has gone on to introduce Social Intelligence [24], others have suggested Creative Intelligence [25], Cultural Intelligence [26] and Spiritual Intelligence [27]. It is in the spirit of these pioneers that I offer AeI© to be explored along with these other forms of intelligence. (See Figure 1.) It is my belief and hope that in this case, more is better because at the core of all our efforts is the vision that talent and aptitude reside within each of us.

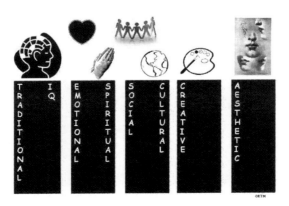

Figure 1

AeI© makes the option of learning from the arts available to all of us, no matter how "unartsy" we think we are. AeI© is a teachable capacity, which can be looked at, studied, and internalized to enhance our capability. Experiencing and replicating the methods of the arts may be fun and inspiring, but this does not in and of itself change behavior. Replicating may invoke original thinking, but what is needed is sustained, original *doing*. Individuals who are not innately attuned to the possibilities of an artistic mindset need more help in learning and adopting new ways of being, knowing, and doing. AeI© makes that possible.

I am specifically steering away from using the word "competency" to discourage what is rampant in most organizations—competency modeling. Though these models may be useful as a framework or for developing a shared language, they tend to perpetuate what author John Katzenbach calls "sameness" and "replication" [28]. These outcomes are in direct conflict with the essence of AeI© and its potential to be expansive and diverse.

AeI© begins with *presence*, the here and now. (See Figure 2.)

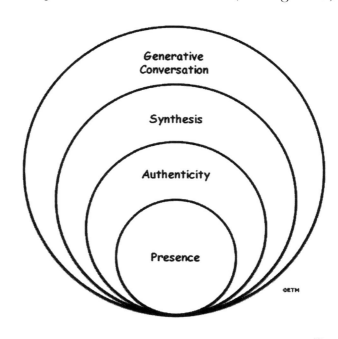

Figure 2

Presence: Being and Acting in the Moment

When I was in grade school, in the 1950s, I clearly remember the morning attendance drill. My teachers would call out our names, and in response, we would say, "present." That is not the kind of present I am talking about here.

Presence is listening intently. Presence challenges us to suspend routine thoughts and allow for the emergent. Presence necessitates that we become aware of ourselves, our innermost thoughts as well as the surrounding environment. With this capacity, we are viscerally in touch with what we are feeling and seek to know why. We witness our impact on others, how others experience us. We recognize, accept, and embrace people and ideas. We are in a state of inquiry, not advocacy or defense. When present, the emergent becomes a source of surprise, energy, connection, inspiration, and creativity. Presence requires that we fully utilize our six senses.

At this point, you may be overwhelmed. This present thing sounds really good, but it also sounds like a lot of work. It is, especially if you are not used to it. However, with daily practice, being present can become your way of being. It can become a mindful habit. *Is it worth it?* If I did not think so, I would have never invested the time and energy to write this book. To see if you think it is worth it, you may have to read on and experiment.

Alan Webber departed the comfort of *Harvard Business Review* to launch *Fast Company*. His words serve to illuminate presence.

> A visual representation of my experience would look like a semi-permeable membrane that keeps accepting signals. Stuff comes through and stuff goes back out, and there's a constant dialogue with your environment. If you're open in relation to your idea, the universe will help you. [29]

These words embody *presence*, availability and accessibility, which are characteristic of an artistic mindset. Webber goes on to say, "Two of the oldest activities in mankind are science and art and both are dedicated to investigating reality. More of both in business would be an asset [29]. No surprise, I agree.

Presence is the "art" of performance. An actor may study a script and internalize every line, but the actor knows that when he or she steps out onto the stage, the other cast members will likely offer something new, something they must accept and respond to on the spot. Actors must accept what they are given. Failing to do so will cause a ripple of unwelcomed events. Actors feel responsible for each other's performance. They expect the unexpected, whether it is a forgotten line or an unrehearsed nuance. They do not want to let another actor, the ensemble, or the audience down. An actor who "phones in" his performance loses respect and trust from the landscape of professionals upon which he relies. Consequently, he loses the right to do the work.

> Michael Spencer, musician, consultant, and educator, states:
>
> Musicians tend to be concerned with the "properties" of what they are listening to when performing on the concert platform, all of it very much to do with creating a sense of good ensemble, to avoid coming in too early, too late, etc. Conversely, business people focus on the "content," the "analysis" of what they are listening to. [30]

This same dynamic echoes all of the performing arts, be it a jazz group or dance company. Artists focus on the whole versus the part. Performance is a constellation of shared efforts and events.

Presence for an actor is not negotiable, but this capacity appears lacking in the business world. I think the lack of presence accounts for a good deal of individual and organizational ailments. The failure to miss cues, large and small, in any given conversation or meeting holds the potential for a range of corresponding consequences. The decision you thought was a "go" proves impotent, as you later discover that no one at the meeting really was onboard. Silence was not agreement. The competitor that snatched onto a new service or product your company chose to ignore. This was the case in the early 1970s when IBM and XEROX dismissed the vision and work of Bill Gates and Steven Jobs and were left with egg on their faces and a monumental catch-up task. (Check out this story in the amazing video, *The Triumph of the Nerds.*). The demise of the Big Three Automakers may have hit the front page in December 2008, but it began decades earlier, when they unilaterally snubbed the threat of smaller and more efficient vehicles made in Japan. Missed cues account for the devastation of the NASA Challenger disaster and the tragedy of 9.11. The list is long, too long, and too familiar.

Performing artists are in the moment, constantly observing, and ready to move. This is most explicit with improvisation, a well-known form of theatre. To the average person, improv appears ad hoc, spontaneous, or as author Malcolm Gladwell claims in his book *Blink*, "utterly random and chaotic" [31]. It is not. Spontaneity in this case is not random or chaotic. Underlying this so-called spontaneity are practiced rules and routines, which enable actors to fully experience the moment. This capacity is exactly what is needed in today's business environment. Our inability to experience in the moment is a major blind spot, which renders us attached to actions and words as if they were carved in stone. C. Otto Scharmer, author and MIT professor, explains, "The blind spot is the place within or around us where our attention and intention originates. It's the place from where we operate when we do something"[32]. Blind spots prevent spontaneity and keep us from being present.

How much of your day truly goes according to plan? Chances are, cancelled meetings, agenda digressions, family emergencies, technology crashes, and the like plague your days. Nearly half a century ago, Henry Mintzberg distinguished between the "folklore and fact" of a typical manager's job [33]. He challenged conventional thinking and texts that preached a manager's job could easily be summed up by four words: plan, organize, control, and lead. Not so! Mintzberg demonstrated that leaders at all levels are interrupted every five minutes—and that was nearly fifty years ago. Add in current technology and it is crystal clear that we work in a time of constant disruption. A recent study estimates that the average worker is interrupted every three minutes [34]. It is a myth that anyone has the luxury of uninterrupted time to think, ponder, and decide. None of us can afford not to be present.

Given this, successful leaders are those who can work without a script. They improvise a lot. They adapt to what is presented to them. They take in the stage and the players; they probe, reflect, and think on their feet. They are engaged with the current dynamic. In a world defined by chaos and complexity, leaders must strategically merge spontaneity with thoughtful reflection to succeed. This demands presence.

It is for this reason, as mentioned previously, that several major companies and medical and business schools have included the art of improvisation in their learning programs. The roots of improvisation go back to the mid-1500s, to the Commedia Dell 'Arts. Performers would engage the audience and play out different scenarios, just as they do today in Second City and other improv venues.

Improvisation provides a forum where actors learn to be comfortable with the unexpected, read others' reactions, agree seamlessly on topics, and create consensus without saying a word. "Effective improvisation requires that no one ever refuses to accommodate the other's work," claim authors Austin and Devin [6]. Consistent with its roots, organizations and schools have looked to this brand of improvisation to cultivate better listening, creative thinking, and adaptive problem solving amongst their population. Improvisation is a medium that offers limitless imagination.

"Yes, And" is a touchstone activity for aspiring actors, designed to strengthen their capacity to be present. It is frequently enacted in corporate and academic programs. Keith Johnstone, author, actor, and teacher, explains, "Good improvisers seem telepathic; everything looks prearranged. This is because they accept all offers made—which is something no 'normal' person would do" [35]. "Yes, And" begins with two people. One person begins a conversation. Anything they say is considered an offer. It may be realistic or outlandish, spontaneous or launched from a given scenario. The other person must respond and follow the four rules of the activity. The respondent must:

> **Accept and develop the story.** This means the actor must respond with a "Yes, And," not a "Yes, But" or a "Yes, Maybe." "Yes" in this case does not mean agreement, but "Yes" does indicate listening. No matter what the lead actor says, the respondent must move the conversation forward by adding new information as opposed to stalling it or adding just filler. The respondent should build, not block or yield. Blocking is a form of aggression, any word or action that prevents the conversation from developing, or weakens your partner's premise. Yielding, passively agreeing without building, does not develop the story.
> **Be in character.** Become the role that is handed to you, for that topic, for that time. There should be no lapses.
> **Be in the moment.** Stay in the situation that is presented. Expect the unexpected. There should be no lapses.
> **Make the other person (or team if working in a group) look brilliant.** All players support one another, no matter what happens. On a team of six, there are five other people whose job is to make the sixth look brilliant.

If you think this is easy to do, it is not. I have conducted this activity with countless groups of corporate and student citizens. It is not easy. The participants struggle with rule one, where they must accept and develop the story. They usually ignore the other three rules completely. I deviate from the normal activity of two people and add another person every five minutes or so. After all, that is what we have in the business world, groups and teams, not just one-on-one conversations. By the time the fourth person is added, the volunteers are vacillating between embarrassment and laughter, their faces begging me to relieve them of their misery.

The debrief of "Yes, And" includes the players as well as the observers. Without exception, prior to the activity, most folks in the room humor me about presence. Not after, when the ramifications of *not* being present surface. Participants find it hard to stay focused, to be disciplined. Drifting is natural, unavoidable. People feel awkward with the uncertainty and fear of looking and sounding foolish. It is hard to really care about what someone else is saying and suspend thoughts and judgments. It is hard for players to respond quickly, cohesively, and in character to possibilities that they do not expect. People act more from assumptions than probing. The notion of making anyone else, yet alone the whole group, look brilliant never registers while struggling to perform yourself. It was not a difficult leap to see that 'out of it' was the norm and that being 'out of it' did not bode well in a business world of shifting landscapes and conversations.

Presence goes beyond the words we and others think and say. Presence demands attention to movement, and movement often determines status. Take a moment and reflect on the various meetings you attend. Think about the room where the meetings are held and the participants there. With that picture in mind, note where people position themselves and how the use of their physical body suggests whether they choose to be close or distant. How we use our body can declare who is up, down, confident, tentative, desirable, or to be avoided. Every movement of the body modifies its surrounding space and the experience of everyone inside that space, causing ripple effects in conversation and relationships. Keith Johnstone captures the power of what cultivated *presence* can offer when he states:

> Once you understand that every sound and posture implies a status, then you perceive the world quite differently, and the change is probably permanent. In my view, really accomplished actors, directors, and playwrights are people with an intuitive understanding of the status transactions that govern human relationships. [35]

Leaders, like actors, directors, and playwrights, are brokers of power, and being capable of recognizing this level of 'noticing' and 'impact' proves valuable. I am reminded of a client I worked with several years ago. He was the CEO and President of a large consumer manufacturing company and called me in to figure out what was wrong with his executive team. According to him, they were tentative, lackluster, and simply not behaving as he expected. This is a typical client situation for me. As usual, my detective work in this instance took the form of interviews and culminated with a team feedback meeting. The evening before the meeting, I met with my client and shared what I had discovered. Predictably, the team members and CEO had entered an implicit collusion to keep each other in the dark, not sharing feedback, and therefore ensuring everyone kept doing just what they were doing. I reported to my client that team members felt he was visibly uninterested in what they had to say, and I cited several examples, such as reading a newspaper while they talked or taking phone calls. By the end of our conversation, my client got the message that he had unintentionally created the lackluster environment he seemed to loathe. The next morning, after the entire team arrived in a familiar boardroom, I asked my client to open the meeting. My client stood and then said something like … "Last night I met with Rochelle, and she shared the feedback we are here to discuss today. You may have noticed I am sitting in a different chair today. This is my way of telling you that I heard the feedback, and I plan to change. I hope you will give me the time to earn your trust again." I had never been in this particular room before, so I was unaware of any seating habits, but now understood why I had noticed a few awkward glances as people arrived earlier. With these few words, my client made a large, impressive, and believable commitment, all because of a change of a seat. Position can speak volumes.

Presence means acting on information in real time. We all know what it is like to be in a situation or with a person and suddenly get a bad taste in our mouth, a queasy stomach, a claustrophobic feeling, a boost of energy, or a blinding headache. These feelings are telling us something. With renewed sensory awareness, these responses to interactions become a source of knowledge and action for self and others. It is to our advantage to know these sources and act accordingly. Short shifting or ignoring these sensual hints usually means unwelcomed surprises down the road. "Don't think about it; feel it. The wisdom in your hands is greater than the wisdom of your head will ever be," whispers the inner voice of Bagger Vance in the film *The Legend of Bagger Vance*. Presence is about learning to trust and acting on these instincts.

Presence determines our aliveness, how available we are to our sense experience. Diane Ackerman eloquently spoke of our potent proprioceptors in her seminal text *The Natural History of the Senses* [36]. Did you know that 70 percent of the body's sense reception resides in the eyes, and it is mainly through seeing the world that we appraise and understand it? Or that we breathe 23,040 times daily and require forty nerve endings to be aroused before we smell something? Or that we have about 10,000 taste buds grouped by theme (salt, sour, sweet and bitter), which are replaced every week to ten days as they wear out?

Touch is ten times more powerful as a means of connecting with others than verbal or emotional expressions. No two of us taste the same apple. Skin has unique pore patterns just like fingerprints and DNA. Our senses are the conveyors of our experiences. They inform our sixth sense, our intuition, our instincts, our gut. Well-cultivated senses help us understand why Malcolm Gladwell declares, "Decisions made very quickly can be every bit as good as decisions made cautiously and deliberately" [31]. To lose touch, *literally* and *figuratively,* is to lose vital information we need to think, decide, and act. We must reclaim this source of connection power and return to experience the textures of life.

What stops us from being present? Mindlessness keeps us a victim of our own social constructs, trapped by categories and premature cognitions. We automatically react from an embedded perspective. "I can't. I shouldn't." We cling to what we have been told and taught or what we have experienced, and these images become photographs where meaning is frozen rather than fluid. We label the intentions of others based on nothing more than etched mental models. "I know who they are; I know what they mean." Linguist David Boehm concludes, "Our thoughts have us rather than we have them" [29]. I feel comfortable asserting that anyone reading this text has silently wondered about the habits of others, whether it was eating french fries with mustard instead of ketchup, having salad after instead of before a meal, donning a specific style of dress or arranging their work spaces and desks. We tend to mindlessly judge rather than explore unfamiliar practices.

In a similar fashion, we respond mindlessly to our environment and daily tasks. Operation by default translates into rote behaviors and attitudes and ensures closed thinking. We think intensively, not extensively. We assign stereotypes to strangers of color, religion, and ethnicity. Our minds become lazy and our opinions immovable. We follow scripts, instead of having present-centered interactions. We stop thinking, feeling, seeing, hearing, and being. As I write, America prepares to inaugurate its 44th president, Barack Obama. This was a campaign and election fraught with etched mental models, people clinging to ways of thinking and doing. The outcome breeds optimism and dramatically displays what can happen when we choose to release ourselves from entrenched thinking.

Moving past our default behaviors and attitudes takes effort. We must start by knowing ourselves. Self-awareness is the first step, and this is a common theme in management and leadership literature. Esteemed management guru Peter Drucker said, "Only when you operate from a combination of your strengths and self knowledge can you achieve true and lasting excellence"[37]. This familiar but timeless wisdom holds true today. Presence demands one must first be self-aware.

Peter Senge claims in his text *Presence* that "the core capacity needed to access the field of the future is presence and that the degree to which we can effectively be present rests on the degree of our self-awareness [29]. Senge's co-author, C. Otto Sharmer, went on to define this process as "presencing" [32]. The ability to sense and connect with the emergent, to a future possibility, demands keen self-awareness, and a key to self-awareness is the willingness to embrace our vulnerability. When I suggest to clients and students that vulnerability is advantageous, they are alarmed. *Won't I lose credibility? I am supposed to know the answers!* These and other comments derive from ingrained socialized messages. In truth, great leaders understand that they do not need to know the answers. They need to know how to ask the right questions. By definition, if one is afraid to be vulnerable, one cannot be present. Cultivating presence means cultivating the ability to suspend our innermost rigid thoughts and judgments. It means not only being comfortable with organic process but also embracing organic process. It means surrendering control of any given conversation and its outcome. This abandonment opens the door to possibilities and redirection. Self-awareness empowers us to course correct in real time. We will talk further about self-awareness later in this book when we discuss systems thinking and alignment.

How can you tell if you are present? You can get a quick glimpse by asking yourself the following questions:

- Do I leave conversations surprised?
- Do I leave conversations energized?
- Do others leave conversation with me surprised and/or energized?

If your answers are not a profound "yes," then it is likely you have room to grow.

To become present is to find a place of "genuine knowing" [29]. To become present is to optimize our senses and challenge the mundane, setting the stage for original, flexible, and timely responses. Presence is not fixed or static, but it evolves, reflecting your own growth and development. This state of being allows us to distinguish what we experience, and it makes the difference between acting with intention in context or responding reactively.

We have a choice in any given moment to be engaged and connect—or not. It seems to me that in times that are characterized by fluctuation, interruption, and rapid change, and when much is unknown and unpredictable, none of us can afford not to be present. Being in touch with the inner places from which we operate in real time may prove to be the differentiating, competitive advantage. The strength of our performance will not be measured with how we responded in the past alone; rather, it will be measured by how we are able to respond to that which has not happened yet. Presence can make the difference between a rapid response and the best rapid response.

Authenticity: Getting in Character with Intention

There are several myths surrounding the term *authenticity*.

The first myth is that you can claim to be authentic. You cannot tell others you are authentic, any more than you can tell others to trust you. Trust is earned. All you can do is ask for the time to earn it. In a similar way, you can strive to be experienced as authentic by knowing yourself and learning to be intentional in the roles that you play. No leader can look into a mirror and say, "I am authentic." Authenticity is a quality that others must attribute to you.

The second myth is that we have a narrow repertoire of authenticity. I have a favorite sweatshirt with the acronym, WYSIWYG ... *What You See Is What You Get*. I resonate with these words because I like to think of myself as the real deal, not a phony. However, there is more to you and me than what others can easily see. The visual is just one view, and it is restrictive. We have more range.

Personality assessments are popular in business, and, like my sweatshirt, they are quick to label and equally restrictive. You are an introvert. Or a chatterbox. A neat freak. Or messy. A logical decision-maker. Or pensive. The personality attributes may be true, but the flaw lies in the interpretation. We are not our personalities. None of us are just one thing or can act one way. This is misleading and often contributes to creating a defensive and self-defeating attitude of "this is me, like it or not." We are rich with a continuum of choices and combinations. The key is to know who you need to be, why, and when.

Think of the wide range of interactions and relationships you have each day: peer, manager, leader, and member. Amongst these roles, you may be asked to facilitate, report, influence, and/or respond. Striving for authenticity forces you to reflect on how you need to be experienced, heard, and seen, and paves the way for you to act with intention to deliver appropriately for each situation. To be authentic builds on being present and requires identifying intentions and assuming the role required to achieve the objective at stake at that time, at that place, and with that audience. Doing this while preserving one's authenticity in the process distinguishes the great from the mediocre leader.

Leaders have much to learn from artists on achieving authenticity. One actor plays many different characters. One musician participates in a range of symphonies. One director rehearses diverse ensembles. And for each role, individuals must bring themselves authentically and deliver the performance for their audience, tapping their vast reservoir of personal experiences and bundling their skill sets appropriately. Artists begin their process by astutely understanding what they bring to a given piece of work and how that will influence their performance. They seek to get inside the character and the meaning behind the script, score, or movement. They draw on their experiences and guard against overstating or compromising the author's intent.

I have a simple but effective way of illuminating this when working in a business setting with groups or individuals. I begin by asking, "What adjectives describe an authentic person?" It usually helps if they think of a specific person in their experience that they regard as authentic. I get predictable responses: integrity, honesty, real, transparent, genuine, etc. Then I ask, "How do you know? What actions do those adjectives translate into? What does this authentic person do or say?" This generates a list of behavioral anchors, such as keeps their word, covers my back, shares information, tells the truth, and the like. The participants then rate themselves on these behaviors as a first step in self-awareness.

During the second part of the activity, I have participants brainstorm a list of situations and stakeholders with whom they work (peer, manager, direct report, client/customer, etc.), and I ask them to identify what their primary contribution or objective is with each stakeholder group (recruit, hire, report, facilitate, influence, persuade, etc.). Then I ask them to hook up with a partner to discuss their lists, focusing on whom they need to be, based on that audience and for that purpose. I encourage them to pose the question for each of their objectives and audiences, "How would I need to be in order to (influence/make a contribution to) my (peers/stakeholder)?" It becomes evident that each scenario calls for something different. The goal of the peer discussion is to reflect and evaluate on how intentional they are and how well they are delivering on those roles. The results are lively and enlightening. One participant found it so eye opening that she assigned metaphors for each of her stakeholders as a mnemonic to trigger her intention and characterization.

All this leads to the definition of authenticity as it relates to AeI©. Authenticity is intentional characterization, thinking and preparing for whom you have to be, for that audience, for that purpose, at that time. Whether it is the good morning salutation, a staff meeting, an executive briefing or a sales call, you must be believable. Pine and Gilmore conclude that "multiple roles are required in today's changing productions" [2]. Becoming intentional—that is, getting into character provides purpose. Like an actor, this is a deliberate process to interact, to perform at the highest level, and it is how you earn the label of being authentic.

Storytelling is a medium of culture for communities of all kinds and has a direct relationship with authenticity. Stories inspire and enroll others. Stories illuminate meaning, data, and direction. They are pathways to understanding. Leaders are often known and remembered for their stories, which reflect their role as organizational sensemakers. To preserve an organization means to preserve its stories. To change an organization means to create new stories. Authenticity is a prerequisite for creating great stories.

Peter Guber, famed producer and writer, eloquently tells us in *The Four Truths of the Storyteller* that storytelling does not conflict with truth but is instead built on the integrity of the story and its teller [38]. Guber reminds us that most stories are to instruct, not entertain. "For the leader storytelling is action oriented—a force for turning dreams into goals and then into results." He offers four truths that leaders can use to govern their storytelling: *Truth to teller, Truth to audience, Truth to moment,* and *Truth to mission.*

Truth to teller means congruency between who you are and what you say. It means generosity and vulnerability. "The spirit that motivates great storytellers is, I want you to feel what I feel," says Guber. Great stories move people to act because they stir hearts and emotions. One example would be Delta Airlines. Post 9.11, Delta fell prey to poor leadership and decision-making, which led to increased low employee morale and sagging customer relations. Delta brought back Gerald Grinstein, a former CEO and a well-liked and effective leader. He had a formidable task. Delta employees at all levels were angry, bitter, and feeling betrayed. They were difficult to negotiate with until rival US Air made a hostile bid to buy out Delta. With that bid, the landscape changed. Now Grinstein's story was not just about money or benefits; it was about pride and identity. Grinstein's story readily embodied his beliefs, took on more meaning and more heart. Within a day or two, thousands of

Delta employees rallied to Grinstein's side and switched positions on several financial issues. The union was now contributing to legal fees to fight US Air, as opposed to funding legal battles with their parent company. That is the power of touching emotions, engaging your audience to feel what you feel. Delta employees had a personal stake in the ground. They gave up whatever their individual desires were at that moment for the *whole*. Whether your story is of crisis or celebration, ongoing or one time, your truth will be determined by the depth of your self-knowledge and intentionality—by your authenticity.

Truth to audience means listeners will feel their time spent listening to you is worthwhile. This demands preparation and understanding what your listeners care about and want to know. It means getting the emotions as well as the facts right. It demands seeking common ground and presenting different faces with different audiences. At first glance, this may seem to fly in the face of what we colloquially associate with authenticity, but it is anything but. Listeners instinctively know when leaders are faking it, and with that, trust will be lost and difficult to recover. In the words of Shakespeare, "All the world's a stage … and one man in his time plays many parts." This is not pretending; this is authenticity.

Truth to moment suggests that content demands reworking because each audience and each time is different. The content is shaped by the context. Truth to mission means everything you say is targeted toward a crystal clear goal and outcome. These four truths underscore the power of intentional characterization, thinking, and preparing for whom you have to be, for that audience, for that purpose, at that time. Together they embody authenticity as an essential element of AeI©.

I had the privilege of working with an amazing leader who provides a terrific example of authenticity in action. At the time, she was the managing director of a global public relations firm, and I had the pleasure of serving as leadership coach for her and her executive team. In time, I worked with everyone in the regional office, from the Vice President of First Impressions (aka receptionist) to the C-Suite. My client was one of the most optimistic and energetic people I have known, a petite powerhouse. It was difficult for an employee to have a bad day around her. Frowns were circumspect. Yet during our time working together, the office confronted a very difficult situation. A mandated office move issued from corporate headquarters left the regional office with inadequate workspaces. Employee morale and productivity simultaneously sank. My client worked hard and worked miracles and within a relatively brief time had the office relocated to a more suitable space. My client had to draw on her range and *intentionally* become the character she needed to be for check signing C-Suite leaders, for the task at hand. To accomplish the task, she needed to be experienced as serious, determined, and credible. For sure, this was a different presentation than the perky leader who showed up every day, warmly greeting her coworkers. Without the ability to cultivate a repertoire of roles, a leader's reach is limited to only those with whom he or she shares common ground.

At the heart of authenticity is learning how to draw from your own well of experiences and behaviors as different situations arise. Like an actor or musician, we must dig deep within ourselves and draw on our history. Leadership expert and author Noel Tichy describes leadership. He says, "Like an actor approaching a new role, the leader must understand the scope of his or her technical skills and then decide what nuance of the role they will highlight" [39]. This depth is only possible when we are able to go beyond the *what* and *how* of our actions and discover the source of our intentions and actions. Characterization is not pretending to be someone you are not; it is being you and being believable in the various roles and scenes with which you engage. It is not manipulation. It is critical versatility; it is deliberate. When a person is authentic, he or she knows the inner source of her actions and is able to extract appropriate characterizations.

Authenticity takes practice, and rehearsal is one powerful means to learn how to enhance it. I do not mean "rehearsal" as in an intense preparation time before opening night. I mean rehearsal to mean cultivating a daily habit of reflection. *Did that meeting go well? Did that conversation yield the intended results or a surprise? What worked and did not work? Was I present? When did I respond reactively, from a default position? What would I do differently if I could rewind the tape? What did I learn about myself, and others, because of that interaction?* Answers to these and other questions help to identify the source of our actions, strengthen self-awareness and inform future interactions.

Rehearsing in this fashion better prepares us to be authentic as we improvise through disruptive days. As said earlier, the best-laid plans give way to spontaneous conversations, debate, and decision-making. We are improvising much more than most of us realize, and the unexpected demands immediate adaptation. Rehearsal offers an ongoing process of continuous improvement, iterative actions of observation and reflection, which bolster our ability to be authentic with intention even in the midst of unpredictable events. Rehearsal makes for "disciplined practicers," whether you are a performing artist or a business leader, and has the power to create memorable performances [40].

Authenticity, intentional characterization, optimizes our interactions, whether they are tacit or explicit. We embrace our various roles with a profound level of knowing and being, which renders our connections meaningful and our messages impactful.

Synthesis: Putting It Together

Synthesis captures the synergy of presence, of being available to access and absorb while being authentically in character. Synthesis is a time of action. Synthesis is felt, heard, and seen. Synthesis has occurred when you leave a meeting with a new idea because the room was percolating with uninhibited participation. It is when you acknowledge, rather than ignore, the veiled yet visible emotions of others. It is when you halt a conversation that suddenly feels wrong before it travels a path of no return. It is when you go with the energy presented, rather than pursue a predetermined course. It is when feedback becomes a common and current behavior, eliminating festering of bad feelings and their destructive consequences. Synthesis occurs when you take the time to reflect on how you contributed to a specific triumph or disappointment. Synthesis is what you do with your experiences and perceptions, disparate or otherwise, to inform thought and action. It is not only being in the here and now, it is acting in the here and now. Synthesis is interdependent with presence and authenticity.

As with *presence* and *authenticity*, the performing artist is a master of *synthesis*. Listening is not the work of one sense but of all the senses: see, touch, taste, smell, hear, and the indefinable and undeniable sixth sense, intuition. Listening is a dynamic, visceral experience, demanding in the moment responses. The musician and actor must respond seamlessly and accurately to what is handed to them. The overall performance is at stake. The high performance businessperson is also a master of synthesis on an individual and collective level, for themselves as well as their organizations.

Consider, for example, that an automobile begins with disparate pieces of metal. Designer couture is shaped from materials of various colors and textures. An Oscar-winning film results from the expert synthesis of snippets into a cohesive and coherent whole. A work of art is a vision coming to life as the palette is dramatically splashed on canvas.

Groundbreaking products are born out of fresh eyes looking to solve common problems. Kodak's flash. Pampers. Swiffer. Post-It Notes. Facebook. Jogging baby carriages. Flex Time. Hot cup holders. TIVO. Velcro. IPhone. HULU. Few of us could imagine life without remote controls, computers, cell phones, and e-mail. Some products change all our lives.

If you think these examples are about creativity, you would be only partially correct. They are about synthesizing new and established ideas in order to be creative and produce innovative ideas, products, and processes. A synthesizer sees underlying patterns and associations beneath the surface and notices what doesn't fit neatly into existing frameworks and mental models. A synthesizer is an innovator, not an opponent of the old, but a proponent of the new. Synthesis is generative, which, in turn, sets the stage for creativity, innovation, and execution.

Although the notion of a creative class culture, as introduced by Richard Florida in his text *The Rise of the Creative Class* may be a unique concept for business, the arts as a peripheral society, has existed for centuries [41]. Theatrical cities were "spectacular" societies, which embodied a cohesion of social, artistic, and political inputs and were characterized by a convergence (synthesis) of ideas. Fast-forward and we see The MacDowell Colony, a 450-acre retreat in rural New England that has served as a creative refuge to over 550 artists of various disciplines since 1907. Designed to respect the creative process, attendees have time and space to interact in an environment free from distractions, where comingling promotes sharing. Since its onset, MacDowell Colony alumni have won more than sixty-five Pulitzers, twelve MacArthur Foundation Genius Awards and claimed scores of Academy Awards, Grammys, Guggenheims, and National Book Awards [42]. This kind of success cannot be ignored.

Let's do the math. Synthesis is a catalyst for creativity; creativity is a catalyst for innovation. Innovation equals growth and economic gain. Conclusion: to achieve and sustain growth, any entity (region, company, institution) must be a place where talented and creative people want to be, a place that provides the infrastructure for experimentation and learning, and welcomes and cultivates diverse ideas and people. It must be a place reflective of the culture of the performing arts.

There is a reason why 98 percent of two-year-olds consider themselves to be creative, while only 2 percent of twenty-five-year-olds hold onto that claim, and the reason is not their potential but the external environment that suffocates the natural tendency for curiosity, play, and exploration. Unfortunately, this tendency for creativity along with our senses is stifled and atrophies over time, producing unimaginative adults who are afraid to think, cross artificial boundaries, and are often intimidated by the unknown or different. Ask an adult to make up a story, and her initial response will be something like "I don't know any" or "What should it be about?" On the other hand, ask a child under five, and he will whip it out in a second. I experience this personally whenever I play with my granddaughters, now seven and five. We do a lot of improvising during our playdates. Making up complex, detailed, multi-character, illustrative stories is effortless for them. Their spontaneity and imagination never cease to amaze me.

The atrophied propensity for creativity becomes an organizational handicap that hinders its capability and performance. Changing this dynamic takes resolve. It takes a stubborn person to remain an artist in a society that values conformity, and it will take the same courage and tenacity of organizations to create a culture where adults can reconnect with their innate aesthetic and creative capacities.

The late economist Mancur Olson noted that the decline of nations and regions is a product of an organizational and cultural hardening of the arteries he called "institutional scleroses" [41]. Unblocking those arteries to unleash creativity and innovation begins with presence and authenticity, employing the full utility of our senses, and the capacity to be poised to synthesize, whether in the arts or business.

Synthesis sets the stage for individual and collective creativity. On a grander scale, synthesis can lead to systemic innovation conceived from daily experiences within cultures designed to foster creativity. Herein lies the dilemma and limitation of organizations attempting to transform their environment with onetime events promising to ignite fresh, unencumbered thinking and creativity. It just can't be done this way. Ideas and behavior that might generate from such isolated experiences will drown quickly in a misaligned cultural environment. As in the world of the arts, for business to reap the benefits of an artistic mindset, it must create and sustain the necessary underlying and embedded supportive mechanisms within its culture. Later in this book, we will look at companies that have done just that and explore ways that you, too, can create a culture of connection, creativity, and innovation.

Synthesis along with presence and authenticity embody the interdependent elements of AeI©. Together these defining elements of AeI© offer individuals and organizations the opportunity to cultivate their artistic mindsets and to fully utilize our six senses in order to spur growth and strengthen performance. The next section further distinguishes how the artistic mindset is a way of being, not doing.

ARTISTIC MINDSET: 'WHEN' NOT 'WHAT'

A mind stretched to a new idea can never go back to its original dimension.
Oliver Wendell Holmes

I tend to be amused by certain distinctions. For example, take the subject Reading. My career began as a reading and language specialist. I worked in various school systems in underserved and disenfranchised neighborhoods. I was struck by how Reading was a separate area of study. I could only wonder what the students were doing the rest of the day in Science, Math, English, and Social Studies. *Weren't they reading all the time?* From my view, the opportunity to learn and internalize effective reading skills was interdisciplinary, not secular. A good reader can choose to be a good reader all the time. The same could be said about dieting, another of my life's endeavors. People who maintain a healthy weight and food regime make exercise and eating well a part of their everyday lives. It is not a special event. It is a mindful choice.

These two examples help distinguish the difference between *when* and *what*. Often, I ask participants what words or phrases come to mind when they think of the words *what* and *when*. At first, I get cross-eyed looks, but after what feels like pulling teeth, I get responses. This is a sampling.

<u>What</u>

- Interrogation, as in *what's* wrong? *What's* that? *What's* the problem?

- An action or tangible, such as he did *what* was expected, we gave *what* we could.

- A noun, an identity or to *what* degree: *What* if! *What* for! So *what*! *What* else!

When

A time, as in *when* will you come, *when* to be silent, since *when*, *when*ever.

What appears more objective. It is a thing, an item, an object, something easily defined, observed, and measured. It seems peripheral to the individual. *What* are you reading? *What* diet are you on? *When* suggests a time, an experience, a feeling. *When* I am reading or eating.

When suggests we *are*, before we *do*. Whereas *what* may be short-lived, *when* feels ongoing.

AeI© is a *when*, not a *what*. Although this concept may sound a bit ethereal, it is an important distinction and one that my early collaborator Constance Goodwin clarified often. AeI© and its elements are not items on a to-do checklist. Rather AeI© is to be internalized, to become a felt way of being and knowing that informs doing. Granted, I recognize that if you are inclined to develop your AeI© it will at first feel clumsy, awkward, and premeditated. However, with practice over time that intentionality will feel less cumbersome. The lasting benefit of internalizing AeI© will be improved relationships, constructive interactions, trust, and respect.

When offers a potent resource in the form of emotional memory. Actors draw on their emotional memory to inhabit the roles handed to them. Learning how to access and utilize emotional memory is standard curriculum for aspiring actors and I believe equally valuable for people in any industry. Recently, I asked a diverse group of MBA students to complete the following activity.

> Go back to a time in your childhood, a welcomed memory. Could be a vacation, special event, or holiday. Something vivid. Revisit that memory (close your eyes, go off to a quiet spot, whatever works). See it. Feel it. Capture it on paper with words and pictures. Note what, who, when, as well as how you and/or others felt. Note how you feel right now, as you revisit it. What aspect of that memory might help you in your role as a leader?

Each class member shares his or her memory and a larger group discussion follows.

Jane remembers a specific challenging Thanksgiving meal. Her mom got sick and was not up to the task of cooking. Jane, then eight, was terrified of not having the traditional Thanksgiving meal at her house. She rounded up both her grandmas, who did not get along, and rallied them to the kitchen. Thanksgiving went off as planned. *Why remember this childhood memory?* Because Jane felt proud. When she told the story, her faced glowed as the joy of that experience was recaptured in real time. I challenged Jane to embrace how she registered that feeling of pride and explore how she can use these feelings to create proud moments with peers and direct reports in her working environment.

John remembers summer holidays at a lake house in upstate New York with his extended family. He tells us how he and his cousins, although very competitive, would wrap towels around their fists and friendly box on the beach. John reflects on that childhood memory and states, "I would like to re-create that sort of healthy culture of competition and friendship should I find myself in a future leadership position."

Emotional Recall allows us to get in touch with feelings and emotions of the past. It is a deeply self-aware experience. Pleasant or not, these feelings and emotions and their accompanying self-knowledge can be drawn upon to inform the present. I often startle folks when I say that we do not miss people; we miss how we feel when we are with them. A lover who makes you feel beautiful. A teacher who makes you feel smart. Children who make you feel silly. A coach who makes you feel competent. Over time, the distinction between the person and the emotion blur, and unfortunately, the loss of the person can mean the loss of the welcomed emotion. It doesn't have to be this way if we recognize that we can tap into our emotional reservoir and use these memories to re-create new relationships and new sources of these vital emotions for those around us and for ourselves. *Who are the actors in your life story and how do they make you feel? How can you tap into that experience today?*

It is this felt sense of being that distinguishes AeI© from a checklist of competencies. The *when* of leadership can be heard as a present leader greets a colleague good morning or addresses key stakeholders. You feel it because they are experienced as authentic by others, whether they are leading an enterprise-wide initiative or a company picnic. You experience it because they absorb, assimilate, and synthesize, acting appropriately whether confronting a crisis, or engaged in a routine conversation.

AeI© cultivates direct sensory knowledge to broaden experience, meaning, and value for self and others. "Are you a *when* or *what* leader?"

GENERATIVE CONVERSATION: GREAT PERFORMANCES REQUIRE GREAT CONNECTIONS!
❖ ❖ ❖

In the new economy, conversations are the most important form of work.
Alan Webber

Language is the human highway, complete with on/off ramps, merges, and other directional choices. Language is our connector at work and play. Our choice of words, tone, rate, inflection, and accompanying movements make the difference between speaking and actually being heard. Regrettably, our ability to effectively connect and converse has been sharply compromised by our increasing reliance on technology and virtual systems. You might say we are suffering from an epidemic of failed communication, which in the view of many shares blame for damaged relationships and lackluster organizational performance.

Language is a pervasive power of culture. It is a spokesperson and storyteller. Human beings are bound together in a speech community. Those who control language, control thought and thereby themselves and others. Language choices influence how energy is used and determine what actions occur. Language is an expression of what is known, and at the same time is organic, a creator of what will be. Familiar words such as ritual or marriage trigger conscious and unconscious ideas with listeners, though not necessarily a shared meaning. Language has the power to literally make reality appear and disappear.

We say what we think. We write what we think. And what we think stems from our experiences, where we have been, what we believe we know and have been taught. I love word games like *Scrabble*, *WordSpot*, *Upwords*, and *Boggle*. These games demonstrate how each of us *sees* differently. If you are not familiar with Boggle, it is a fast moving competition. Two or more people sit with pad and pen in hand. A container with a clear cover holds sixteen cubes. Each cube has one letter etched on each of its four sides. One person shakes up the container causing the sixteen cubes to fall randomly into the available sixteen slots. At that time, the three-minute timer is set and players study the letter formation searching for words that are at least three letters (to qualify as a word, the letters must be sequential, horizontally or vertically). I approach this game with a vengeance, cowering over my pad as if I were taking a competitive exam. When times is up players share their lists, and get to keep only those words that no one else has identified. Without exception I am stunned by the number of common words I missed that my opponent has listed. My competitors experience a similar 'duh' surprise. Boggle illuminates the tacit boundaries of our thinking. We all do *see* things differently. Our actions emanate from our view of the world and our place in it.

It is for this reason that none of us can take for granted that the words we utter are heard and processed as we intend. Or that the meaning we assign to words we hear accurately captures the intent of others. More often than not, our intentions and outcomes do not match.

We have all heard or spoken the following cries of frustration at one time or another:

- You don't understand!
- You are not listening!
- Stop interrupting!
- Get to the point!
- You're overreacting!

These are the audible expressions. More devastating and equally rampant are the silent statements of disappointment, fear, omission, misunderstanding, and anger that compromise relationships on every stage. Communication need not be successful to have occurred. Just as in tennis, you may win or lose a match, but in either case, you have played tennis. When we cry, *We are not communicating!* - we are indeed communicating. Whether we do so effectively or not, is another matter.

Enter, *Generative Conversation*. Where there exists an artistic mindset, there follows generative conversation. Generative conversation is emergent and begins with deep listening. Instead of preparing our response, we are *present,* absorbing the complete landscape: self, others, movement, tone, surroundings. We are in character, *authentic* for that time, purpose, and audience. Good questions facilitate probing, decoding the true message and in turn encourage a *present* and *authentic* response, in lieu of an automatic response. Conversations are more robust and less adversarial. We notice more and therefore have more to work with. *Synthesis* interweaves the ingredients of our experience and ensures action in real time. Generative conversation reflects one's ability to be *present, authentic,* and to *synthesize* - the fundamental elements of AeI©.

Generative conversation embodies the attributes of what Roger Martin, author and Dean of the University of Toronto's Rotman School of Management calls "integrative thinking", the subject of his text, *The Opposable Mind.*

> Integrative thinking is the ability to face constructively the tension of opposing ideas and, instead of choosing one at the expense of the other, generate a creative resolution of the tension in the form of a new idea that contains elements of the opposing ideas but is superior to each. [43]

Martin contends that integrative thinking is a consistent attribute of great and bold leadership and provides several notable examples to illuminate his theory. Pioneer Martha Graham established Modern Dance, a powerful, integrated and holistic venue in the face of conventional dance practice. "For Graham, composition, choreography, costumes, and sets were all part of an interdependent, integrated whole."[43] In doing so, she revolutionized an art form. Hotelier, Isadore Sharp, insisted on creating a hotel that could both offer the intimacy of a small motor inn and the amenities of a large convention hotel. His tenacity and commitment to finding a better, not easier solution, took the form of the renowned *Four Seasons* properties. It takes generative conversation to navigate integrative thinking, to be open to explore, and available for surprise in order to synthesize unconventional outcomes.

How we use language to inform our connections and conversations has the power to create camaraderie or conflict, progress or regression, connection or abandon. In this global and virtual world, communication has become a mindless habit, absent connection and conversation. Consequently, messages can be terse, excessive, misinterpreted, or laden with emotional undercurrents. Today, more than ever, organizations are challenged to create generative spaces and mechanisms that facilitate conversations which spark imagination, creativity, and energy - all of which is required for collaboration and innovation essential to tackle the fast pace of learning and problem solving which defines today's business environment. In short, great performances require great connections, and electronic, distant, immediate communication does not suffice. For the most part, they do not create generative spaces.

This is especially true when you consider that only seven percent of our messaging resides in our words. Fifty-five percent of our message is shared by our body language, movements, and gestures (eye contact, fiddling with stuff, leaning toward or away from) and thirty-eight percent by paralinguistics (voice quality, tone, pace, volume). I call this the *Power of the 93%*, deeming electronic communication woefully inadequate. An *Aesthetically Intelligent* person will attend to all three elements of connection – words, movement and voice – noticing and addressing incongruence in real time. When an employee says, "fine" but their body language says, "I am stressed", the person will respond appropriately. When a colleague says "I agree", but their tone says, "No way!" the dissonance will be surfaced, not avoided. Creating generative conversation does take more time and effort than rapid texting or email, but I believe that the potential rewards reaped from great connections justify the investment.

Communication as a general term may be appropriate for sharing information and data, but for the purposes of AeI© falls short as a means of connection. There is a *qualitative* distinction between communication and the experience of connection.

How people connect with each other at work reflects their culture. *Are employees intimidated and as such hold back information? Or, are they encouraged to dialogue, in a culture of candor, openness and informality?* Leaders define culture and set the tone and manner for how employees connect. Ralph Kerle, Director of the Creative Leadership Forum, describes the mandate for leaders today when he says, "If the output of a musician is music, the output of a playwright a script, the output of a sculptor is a piece of visual art, then the output of a leader is creative conversation." Language choices can make the difference between spawning collaboration and innovation or stifling and retarding organizational effectiveness. It may be that some people innately possess effective language skills. However, whether knowingly or otherwise, the elements of AeI© and the skills of generative conversation can be cultivated. All it takes is the choice to do so, individually and organizationally.

It is not by accident that Google is an "innovative ecosystem."[44] It is by design, that Google remains a talent magnet while setting the standard for twenty-first productivity and growth. A core aspect of their organizational design focuses on connection. Beyond the massive intranet and global networks, Google is intent on employees learning from others inside and outside of the company. Offices are designed to facilitate employee exchanges, building on the work of icons like Herman Miller and Intel. Outlets on stair landings accommodate spontaneous sharing and dialogue. All hands meeting take place every Friday. Tech Talks are given by distinguished researchers to a diverse employee audience.

Pixar is another organization that has consciously created an environment of connection. For example, they established a 'Braintrust', a safe forum for less experienced directors to explore early ideas and gain feedback from seasoned directors and leaders. Daily feedback and post mortem sessions ensure final work is on target. Pixar designed their physical space to encourage comingling. Common needs areas such as the cafeteria and post office are centrally located, traversed by all. More on Pixar when we discuss culture.

Google and Pixar no doubt were inspired by W.L.Gore & Company, an amazing model of sustained creativity and innovation success. W.L.Gore is a privately held organization best known for Gore-Tex fabrics, Glide dental floss and Elixir guitar strings. It employs over 6300 people and sells over 1000 products and since its inception in 1958, it has enjoyed double-digit annual revenue growth. No easy feat. W.L.Gore is a campus of inconspicuous close-knit small buildings with no more than 200 employees per building. Each building houses a mix of R&D, Marketing, Sales, and Finance employees. There are no fancy labs. Entire teams work together. Roles blend. Interdependency is cultivated. People pursue ideas on their own, connect with one another, and collaborate out of self-motivation rather than obligation. Ideas are not ghettoized. The gems of this kind of dynamic collaboration are born out of moment-to-moment interactional dynamics. Gore's organizational design intentionally inspires access, connection, and spontaneity to allow for the emergent. This kind of environment fosters ongoing, consistent, breakthrough creativity and innovation. W.L. Gore has indeed created a spectacular *peripheral* society, and we will revisit this stellar company during our culture discussion.

Although historically electronic communication has been inadequate, we are beginning to see enhanced applications. As I write, we have an excellent example of how technology can be used to build connections. Regardless of political affiliation, most people agree that President Barack Obama ran an incredible campaign on every level. A significant aspect of his extraordinary success was the way he used technology to reach out and touch people across gender, generation, and demographics. He continued to use technology during his transition as a tool of inclusion, airing videos that were conversational and invited the viewer to respond with questions, comments, and ideas. Viewers were encouraged to vote on the most urgent questions to help the new administration determine priorities. President-Elect Obama aired weekly videos to keep people informed and involved. The entire website www.change.gov was designed with interaction in mind. Within minutes of Obama's inauguration, the administration launched www.thewhitehouse.gov, a mammoth website to expand the dialogue, educate, and provide transparency. These efforts complemented, not replaced face-to-face connections, and demonstrate how the tools that distance us can also be used to bring us closer together.

Some may argue that sites such as *Facebook* and *LinkedIn* forge connections and generative conversation and to some degree that is true. However, terse comments and often one-way encounters dominate those sites and these types of interactions do not qualify as generative conversation as defined in this book.

Generative conversation as a medium of AeI© demands intentional *presence, authenticity* and *synthesis*. With generative conversation, we consume experiences, not things, assuming the posture of a performing artist who approaches their work with an assumption of what can be, not what is. An actor once casted will study the character he or she will play, but will enter rehearsal understanding those notions will evolve as the ensemble weaves their words and movements to tell a story. The operative question framing this experience is, "What could be?" In contrast, business players often come to meetings and decision-making with an end in mind that they are willing to defend and fight for. The operative statement framing this experience is, "What should be!" (Table 1.) This type of response, firmly rooted in most organization, is inadequate and proves unsuccessful in a fast paced, competitive environment where the game and the players are always changing. Generative conversation leads to what Roger Martin dubs, *Generative Reasoning*, characterized by a leap of mind rather than adhering to traditional deductive and inductive logical methods. These are the tools of creative exploration and resolution.

Should Be	Could Be
Stagnate Thinking	Routine Rethinking
Sparse Reflection	Disciplined Practicer
Singular View	Shared Orientation
Don't Rock the Boat	Deliberate Interruption
Communication	Conversation/Connection
Static Collaboration	Dynamic Collaboration
Self-Centered	Self-Interest and Interdependency
Uncertainty Angst/Fear of Failure	Uncertainty Certain/Embrace Risk
Casted Roles	Taking Turns
Limited Person Engagement	Passion, Pride, and Energy
Defending Positions	Spontaneity

Table 1

Generative conversation posits that conversation is a process that changes us, others, and situations. Change may be hardly noticeable or significant, but it is always there. Generative conversation is a catalyst for creative dialogue as it chips away at entrenched mindsets. People move beyond the past to embrace the possible. It is intentional and emergent, grounded and flexible. Learning how to create more effective connections is power—power to influence, power to align intentions and outcomes, and power to feel good about our conversations and have others feel good too.

The easiest way to initiate Generative conversations is to adopt a *Present - Could Be - Yes, And* attitude through language choices. Simple phrases such as the ones suggested below (See Table 2.) demonstrate that we are paying attention and noticing, and serve to open up the dialogue and create an environment of inquiry, not advocacy. Absent generative conversation, defensiveness leaves us unable to learn anything that opposes our current thinking and sharply lessens the possibility of creative solutions.

Generative Conversation Phrases

Are there other ways we can do this?	Let's try.
What if... (play with perspectives).	I notice that you seem (confused, etc.).
Tell me more.	Go on. Continue.
What other options are there?	And then?
How else can we think about this issue?	You appear (tense, pleased, etc.).
What is the opposite of this thinking?	Seems interesting.
We might want to consider...	How did you come to think that way?
I follow what you are saying...	Yes, hmmm...
How did you come to believe that...	How do your thoughts complement and/or conflict my point of view?
RTM©	

Table 2

We rise to high levels when we develop strong connections. We participate and encourage meaningful dialogue. Whether one-on-one or organization wide, generative conversation engages people's hearts as well as their minds and focuses on interactions (employee, customer, stakeholder, and shareholder) while delivering desired results.

Great performances require great connections!

INTERLUDE...A SYSTEMS PERSPECTIVE

*No one can whistle a symphony. It takes
an orchestra to play it.*
H.E. Luccock

Actions speak louder than words! It is easy for anyone, including me, to espouse intriguing ideas, but it is not so easy to accomplish changes to how we think and behave or how our organizations look and act. Individual change demands personal work, profound self-awareness and a willingness to confront the pieces and parcels of ourselves that we would rather ignore. Organizational change demands a clear understanding of how the elements of an organizational system work, the congruency of its parts and people, and a commitment to creating and sustaining collective alignment.

It is not possible to be present without knowing oneself. Presence requires a keen inner radar that is equally attuned to noticing what is happening internally as well as externally. Before we can intentionally assume diverse roles, we must first know ourselves and be comfortable in our own skin. Authentic leaders know where they come from and who they are, and they know how to use their backgrounds to build connection with others. Self-awareness is how we earn the right to enroll and influence others, to build purposeful legacy organizations.

The following section is an interlude, an intermission of sorts to offer thoughts on how to begin the process of self and organizational knowledge. These may be viewed as two interdependent systems that when mutually aligned comprise the prerequisites for being Aesthetically Intelligent and embedding Aesthetic Intelligence in your organization. Although my focus is on AeI©, this section is application neutral. That is to say, it does not matter what individual and/or collective learning and change you are considering; self and organizational knowledge are required. To proceed otherwise is to ensure compromised results.

WE ARE OUR STORIES

※ ※ ※

Leadership is an intense journey into yourself. You can use your own style to get anything done. It's about being self-aware. Every morning, I look in the mirror and say; I could have done three things better yesterday.
Jeff Immelt, CEO, General Electric

Earlier we discussed the power of stories, and in this section we delve further into storytelling and how it specifically can deepen our self-awareness. The stories we tell, whether they embody a play script, a company forum, or a casual encounter, reflect us and have the power to shape others. Stories define relationships, trigger events, and establish priorities. Stories of identity convey values, create role models, and reveal how things work. Stories describe societies and serve to invite and orient new members. In words and pictures, stories record history, capturing memories for all of time.

In her article, "I Am My Mother's Daughter," Nancy Adler vividly describes a personal revelation after her mother told her the story of Nancy's great-grandmother's selfless acts during the Holocaust in World War II. Nancy's grandmother confronted a difficult, heinous choice of safely leaving Austria with her children or remaining with her parents. This agonizing decision was made by her grandmothers, who pleaded, "Leave! If you don't, our family has no hope of surviving. Leave! For your sake, for the children's sake, and for the sake of the children! Leave!" [45] Nancy shares how she came to see how this act of sacrifice informed the person and the leader she became.

Each of us has a similar story; however, few of us take the time to reflect on our roots and how they shape our adult attitude and behaviors. This is a missed opportunity, for within our stories resides the insight to understand and inform current thoughts and action. Howard Gardner calls these, *Identity Stories,* the roots of our personal experiences, the landscape that shapes all aspects of our life. I might even be so bold as to say that knowing our stories is beyond opportunity; it is an imperative for living life completely and courageously. Whether you choose to cultivate your AeI© or not, strengthening your self-awareness will serve you well.

The following are two autobiographical activities I use to facilitate such reflection in business and student group sessions. I invite you to experiment.

In bits and pieces, participants view the film, *A Chorus Line,* and this proves more compelling than mere entertainment. The script unravels individual stories, revealing shared universal emotions and lasting impacts of family baggage. I am particularly drawn to the character Paul when he says, "Who am I anyway? Am I my résumé?" Regardless of profession or industry, I suspect we all have wondered similar human thoughts and had the same self-doubts. The sixteen final chorus line candidates ultimately disclose their stories and family sagas, sharing tales of abandonment, uncertainty, passion, disappointment, optimism, and hope. After viewing the film, the session participants engage in robust discussion, sharing observations and reactions. They are usually surprised by the meaningfulness and human dynamics the cast and script offer. Following group discussion, I ask participants to reflect on their personal history, to note the key players and critical events that they believe have defined them, and write down how that history manifests itself in their various roles today. The voluntary sharing that follows is rich with heightened self-awareness. This type of activity calls attention to the anchors of our identity and serves as a catalyst toward knowing ourselves. The narrative of our life provides the context for our experiences.

In another activity, I ask participants to complete the following assignment.

> Illustrate the *'professional'* you - how you are experienced by others as a leader and as a member with various stakeholders (managers, direct reports, clients, external partners). Illustrate what you think you do well, or not so well. As the author, you decide on the level of disclosure.
> When finished...
>
> - Place a checkmark (✓) next to things that feel good, work well and you want to keep.
>
> - Place a (?) next to anything that seems like a surprise, or that you do not understand about yourself.
>
> - Place a thumbs down sign (👎) next to things you are not pleased with, things about yourself that you might want to modify.
>
> Post your illustration around the room in preparation for group sharing.

I provide a single piece of flip chart paper for each individual and a table covered with all kinds of artistic mediums—markers, cloth, paper towel rounds, wrapping paper, pipe cleaners, feathers, muffin cups, buttons, and other assorted decorative options—the very same arts and crafts I keep around for playing with my delightful granddaughters.

This activity begins with awkwardness. Limiting adults to illustration and not allowing them to use words is tantamount to tying their arms behind their backs. Asking them to be enthusiastic about doing something they associate with preschool feels odd. A tentative paralysis sets in, but it does not last long.

Within minutes, the artist within emerges. There is audible and visible energy as the adults choose and position crafts. Thoughtfulness as they create their masterpiece. Boldness as they place it on the wall. However, the best is yet to come when they begin to tell their story, bringing life and meaning to the forms and shapes on the paper. (See Figure 3.) The telling is a time of reflection, disclosure, and, sometimes, epiphany. Illustrating forces people to utilize atrophied senses and tap into their innate artistic mindset. Creating and sharing the story often exposes that which may have been unknown. Sources of frustration and pride as well as gaps between intention and outcomes are illuminated. Group conversation offers storytellers new insights and perspectives.

We Are Our Stories

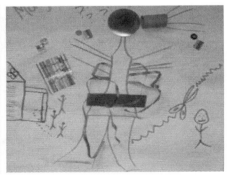

Figure 3

These activities work to deepen self-awareness. As Nancy Adler states, "The more clearly we understand the roots of our identity and humanity, the more able we will be to use our strengths and core values to achieve the vision we have for ourselves and the world around us" [45]. Becoming aware of our stories strengthens our self-awareness by heightening our visceral connections. It helps us better understand the rules we impose on ourselves and how each of these rules becomes a bar in cages of our own design, stagnating our potential to reflect, grow, and change.

Seeking and synthesizing feedback is an additional way to become self-aware. Feedback may be formal, as in a 360-multirater tool, or it may be gleaned informally through observation and probing. The key to optimizing any feedback, welcomed or not welcomed, is to synthesize themes and gain a clear understanding of what behavior and actions (what you do and what you say) account for the feedback. Too often we accept the feedback at face value, fail to probe further, act on assumptions, and subsequently make unilateral decisions about how to remedy the situation. That is unfortunate because the givers of feedback are usually the best people to help you figure out what to do—whether that means modifying a behavior or perhaps reframing a perception. Feedback is not a directive to do things differently; it is an invitation to learn more about how you are experienced by others, to help you identify gaps, and inform how you might modify your behavior.

Feedback and journaling go hand in hand. I ask my coaching clients to keep a journal. I am not fussy. I don't care if the journal is a handsome leather bound book or a bunch of post-it notes. The purpose of the journal is to capture unfiltered visceral responses, in the moment responses to people and situations. Journaling this way provides real-time discussion data, which, over time, surfaces themes and sources of self-awareness. Journaling combined with various feedback methods offers the most reward when it becomes an ongoing activity, a way of being as opposed to a short-lived exercise. Management icon Peter Drucker sought and tracked feedback for decades during his long, rewarding career, claiming it took several years before he accumulated enough meaningful data to understand himself and modify his behavior accordingly [37].

To know ourselves is to know our stories, our roots, our strengths, opportunities, and values. We must learn how others experience us, confront our habits and assumptions, and determine what can or needs to be different. Authentic leaders invest the time to know their stories. Authentic leadership emerges from this keen self-awareness. Leadership authors Kouzes and Posner proclaim in their text *Credibility* that "to be a credible leader, you must first clarify your own values, and the standards by which you choose to live your life" [46]. Phil Mirvis, noted author, professor, and psychologist, considers this personal inner work essential for leaders, "whether in the form of reflection, meditation, prayer or journaling, all of which can deepen one's sense of self" [47]. Peter Senge concurs, "This inward-bound journey lies at the heart of all creativity, whether in the arts, in business, or in science." These comments are consistent with a 2007 study by *Harvard Business Review*, which reported that when seventy-five members of the Stanford Graduate School of Business were asked to identify the single most important capability for leaders to develop, their answer was nearly unanimous—self-awareness [48].

Astute self-awareness poises us to more fully engage with our environment, to observe, to absorb, and to allow for the emergent. It helps us identify points of compatibility or conflict with the larger systems with which we interact: our families, work environment, and community. The depth of our self-awareness correlates to the depth of our learning, and therefore our subsequent actions. Self-exploration is the reflective partner of lives in progress.

Self-awareness ignites our senses and nurtures intense alertness. Self-awareness prepares us to be present and authentic in our various interactions, able to synthesize and act in the moment. Self-awareness empowers us with choices and is a first step to cultivating our AeI©.

THE ORGANIZATION: INSIDE, OUTSIDE, AND IN THE MIDDLE

There are no maps, only compasses.
Anonymous

We move from the system of self to the system of an organization.

Although the literature describing the labels and arrangement of organizational elements—be it a for profit or nonprofit entity—may vary, most would agree on some basic building blocks. (See Figure 4.)

Elements of an Organizational System

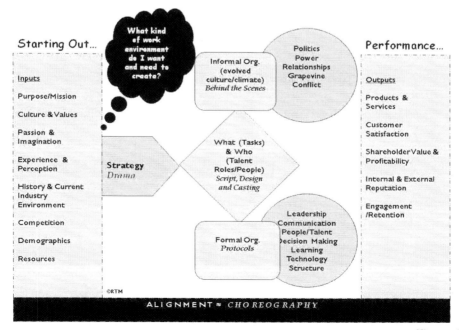

Figure 4

Starting Out - *Inputs* (purpose/mission, culture and values, passion and imagination, experience and perception, history and current industry environment, competition, demographics and resources). *What purpose do we serve? What passion or idea is driving us? What is our history? What kind of work environment do I want and need to create? Will our culture help or hinder our performance? Who is our competition? What will be our competitive edge? What is the economic climate? What is the current pulse of our target market? What resources are required to build our entity?* These answers inform;

The ***Strategy*** – The *drama*, the central *playbook* that brings to paper the blueprint for success and in turn determines *script* and *design*;

The ***What***, *tasks* that must be done and the ***Who***, the *cast* to do it (talent, roles and people) which identify the *how*;

The ***Formal*** *Protocols* and policies such as Leadership and Team Development, Communication, People/Talent Management (Recruitment, Selection, Performance Management, Promotion Succession Planning, Compensation), Decision Making, Learning, Technology, Organizational Structure (Chain of Command, Span of Control) and ***Informal*** *Behind the Scenes* mechanisms, the unwritten rules of behavior that dictate how things really work (politics, power, relationships, grapevine, conflict). These processes facilitate accomplishing our tasks and come together to create;

The ***Performance*** - *Output* (products and services, customer satisfaction, shareholder value and profitability, internal and external reputation, and engagement/retention) which will be judged by the respective *audience* to generate feedback to drive continuous improvement.

As you can see, organization design tells a story, a series of questions and answers that materializes as a tangible picture capturing the explicit and implicit purpose, process, and outcome of any given entity. Be it a business enterprise or performing arts ensemble, success depends on the harmony of every person at every level. Success results from a blending of efforts that taps into the inherent energy and unique skills of its members, demanding each person stay aware of how his or her work aligns with that of their fellow performers. This dynamic is as true for IBM as it is for the ensemble of *A Chorus Line*. Much of what goes on inside goes completely unnoticed by the ultimate customer, the audience, as the front and back of the house contribute to create a seamless experience. However, here is where there is a distinct fork in the road between business and the arts. Bob, set designer, sums up how alignment works in the arts when he says, "Everyone knows the dance." Whereas a shared mission, collaboration, and interdependency are firmly rooted in the culture of the performing arts, these attributes appear elusive for many companies.

The ingredients of an organizational system may be obvious, but creating and sustaining alignment is not. Every aspect of an organization must be aligned with the mission in order for the organization to operate and perform as desired. Too often, leaders seek to inject change into their organizations without properly assessing all the parts and processes that must be modified accordingly. Nadler and Tushman write that "a system is a set of interrelated elements which ultimately produce behavior patterns and in turn, organizational performance—a change in one element affects other elements" (48). Like a pebble tossed into a pond, a change in any one element will cause ripple effects elsewhere. Achieving and maintaining organizational alignment requires ongoing attention. It is indeed effortful.

Whether that change is creating a culture of connection and creativity, modifying leadership behavior, altering a performance management process, or reorganizing the organizational chart, it is critical to know that introducing any change puts into motion domino effects elsewhere.

As much as I hope that you, the reader, will be inspired to embed AeI© in your organizational system, I caution against change without proactive alignment assessment. One size does not fit all. What is successful in one place will not necessarily work at another. This is why many organizations failed miserably when they sought to adopt a facet of the GE Way. They envied GE results and were inspired by CEO Jack Welch, but they fooled themselves into thinking they could get the same results by adopting a sampling of methods and investing a snippet of his commitment and resources. Misalignments compromise an organization's intention and performance.

When we talk about AeI© in Action, bear in mind the elements of an organization. If you choose to change or lead change, do so with the system in mind. The next section continues to discuss why alignment is an imperative, not an option, and offers insight gleaned from the performing arts on critical alignment factors.

ALIGNMENT: DESIGN AND PERFORMANCE

Other things being equal, the greater the total degree of congruence or fit between the various components, the more effective will be the organization.
David Nadler

I live close to the Chattahoochee River, and when I take a walk or ride my bicycle, I pass the rowing club. Rowing is an ideal metaphor for alignment.

Rowing is a symphony of motion. The symphony is not one of competition, but of harmony over water, a movement of wood and muscle, where each piece of equipment and every oarsman is both essential to and the limit of the motion itself.

A coxswain, a coach who determines the pacing and steers the course of action, guides the rowers. Winning will be dependent on how well each rower strokes powerfully and consistently with all the others as well as how the team responds to changes in external influences such as weather.

Organizations, like rowing teams, rely on the coordination of the heart, mind, and muscle of their members. And like rowing teams, their success will depend on their ability to respond quickly and correctly to changes in external influences.

Alignment in an organization refers to the synergy, the integration of people and parts, formal and informal processes, to achieve performance toward the stated purpose, the mission of the business. I emphasize that alignment is subjective. It is not a best in class goal, but rather, it is measured by how well outputs match intended strategy. Unfortunately, as simple as it is to define it, alignment has proven hard to achieve and harder to sustain. After twenty plus years as an organizational consultant, I can comfortably say that rampant misalignment plagues most business organizations. No matter what an organization does or hopes to do, the result will be compromised by misalignments.

On a small scale, organizations experience daily misalignments in communication and process, spawning conflicts between the back and the front of the house, headquarters and the field. There are misalignments in words and action: a company says one thing yet does another. There are misalignments between the standards by which people are measured and what they are told to do. A company promises good service but fails to employ enough people to deliver on it, or it fails to empower them with the education they need to actually provide good service. The root of misalignment can often be found as gaps between formal and informal processes, rhetoric and behavior. The consequences can be disenfranchised employees, missed deadlines and failed products, or reprehensible outcomes, such as the demise of Wall Street and the collapse of an entire financial sector. The tales of great strategy derailed by poor execution are all too common. Alignment is frequently disrupted by lone rangers, silo mentality, competitiveness, narrow decision-making, and unintended ignorance.

So What! *Why should you care?* Because misalignments cost money! In my business we have a saying: "Pay now (for preventive, proactive planning), or pay later (after the fact)." The point is that if you fail to assess, design, and align your organization around your mission and strategy, you will pay the cost of disappointing results and rework. This helps to explain why The Wharton School and similar studies report that nearly 85 percent of all mergers and acquisitions fall short of their objectives, a consequence of inadequate due diligence. What is more disturbing is that 80 percent of these companies studied thought they had achieved success [49]. Ignorance is not always bliss!

In Atlanta, I have watched the sad demise of The Home Depot under Bob Nardelli's reign. The Home Depot was my first client after I moved to Atlanta. Nardelli came in and broke every rule in leading change. Countless misalignments erupted—the way work was done, how employees were treated, excessive pay, lack of community involvement—all of which were out of sync with the mission and reputation Bernie Marcus and Arthur Blank strove to achieve. The result was a disengaged community of customers and employees, and glaring gaps between an espoused culture and reality, culminating with a publicized, expensive exit of Nardelli and others. It remains a question as to whether The Home Depot will ever regain its footing.

Kaplan and Norton conclude in their text *Alignment,* "Understanding how to create alignment in organizations is a big deal, one capable of producing significant payoffs for all types of enterprise" [50]. No doubt, organizations have changed a great deal since the Industrial Age, and expansive global outreach and virtual networks add to the challenge of creating and sustaining aligned enterprises. However, the cost of inaction far outweighs the effort. Insights from the world of the arts can be helpful in reminding us what is core to achieving alignment.

Both an ensemble and a business have a mission. Mira Hirsch claims, "Theatre is a uniting passion with a common goal to create the most effective piece of theater we can." An ensemble's mission, then, is to tell a writer's story; a company's mission such as The Home Depot's was to change the home improvement industry with warehouse stores and provide unrivaled customer service.

My experience with theatre is that everyone arrives at the set onboard; they implicitly know why they are there without being told. As mentioned earlier, there are no mission statements on the wall, pep rallies or leaders goading them to be excited. Actors passionately share a focus on telling the writer's story, the overall ensemble performance, not their individual performance. They intrinsically know their performance is intimately dependent on everyone else. This is equally true for those behind the scenes. Blake Hall, actor and director, sums it up, "Everyone has the same goal. Everyone has their eye on the same prize."

In contrast, if you walked the halls of most corporate offices and asked employees what their contribution is or what they are working for, they would likely tell you their job title, distinct from the organization's mission. I strongly suspect few in The Home Depot today even know what their original mission was. Organizations are notorious for putting on road shows, strategy meetings, and all kinds of things to engender excitement and commitment. They do so with the best of intentions and often with marginal results.

Actors and technical staff in the performing arts do not align easily because they lack courage or conviction. They do so because they love what they do, and they know they need everyone else around them in order to do the work they love. Without exception, every actor and technical staff person with whom I met told me they loved their job. The playwright's story is more important than any one actor's respective part. They exude pride at being a part of theatre's mission, serving as a catalyst for learning, change, and entertainment.

The world of performing arts shows us that organizational alignment is intimately dependent on individuals' alignment with the greater mission. Therefore, the golden nugget for business is the link between individual engagement, organizational alignment, and overall performance.

> **Individuals ➢ Energy ➢ Alignment = Collective Energy & Performance©**

Organizations are made up of individuals with energy to expend. Organizational energy is the force with which a company functions. Mindful design of systemic elements garners this energy and translates it into organizational performance. Organizational members breathe life and legacy into their work, and the energy exhibited is palpable. Individuals do not want to disappoint the whole group, the whole entity. This immersion is what happens in a theatre ensemble when individual egos disappear in the context of the play or production. The critical mandate for leadership anywhere is to ensure individual engagement with the overall organizational purpose. I recently read an article in which now President Obama's explains why his transition team was so effective.

> I don't think there's some magic trick here. I think I've got a good nose for talent, so I hire really good people. And I've got a pretty healthy ego, so I'm not scared of hiring the smartest people, even when they're smarter than me. And I have a low tolerance of nonsense and turf battles and game playing, and I send that message, as opposed to personal ambition or grievance. If you've got really smart people who are all focused on the same mission, then usually you can get some things done. [51]

The leadership capability to play to your strength, coupled with demanding that everyone is on the same page is critical to success. Collins and Porras echo this in their text *Good to Great*:

> Leaders translate their core ideology into every aspect of their organization - goals, strategies, tactics, policies, processes, cultural practices, management behaviors, building layouts, pay systems, accounting systems, job design - into everything that the company does. The company creates a total environment that envelops employees, bombarding them with a set of signals so consistent and mutually reinforcing that it is virtually impossible to misunderstand the company's ideology and ambitions. (*Alignment*) may be the most important point to take away from this book, and by alignment, we mean simply that all the elements of a company work together in concert within the context of the company's core ideology and the type of progress it aims to achieve. [52]

To create an Aesthetically Intelligent organization, one that is collaborative, creative, and innovative, requires alignment in all facets of the organizational system. Here is an example.

There was a time when a beauty salon was a noisy, bustling, relatively small space packed with women in curlers, adorned by large metallic hair dryers and lots of chatter. Not anymore. Today, salons are designed to create an experience. Smooth jazz replaces verbal din. Mirrors and chairs are tastefully placed. Herbal aromas and scented soaps heighten the senses. Increasingly, men populate salons with equal engagement, rendering gender specific salons obsolete. But some things do not change. There are the owners. The reception people. The washers. The master cutters. And the go fors. The class lines at most salons are as striking as any large professional services firm.

Enter my hair salon, Aria.Salon.Spa.Shoppe, an Aveda Lifestyle Salon. I, like many folks, am attached to the person who touches my hair. In my case, that would be Mechelle, who just knows what I need when it comes to my hair. Over the years, I have watched Mechelle and her husband, Matthew Khodayari, move from working for someone, to opening their own salon in Alpharetta, Georgia, a suburb of Atlanta. Getting a haircut and color leaves a lot of available time to observe. I am often a fly on the wall, watching with awe and amazement. There are no silos at Aria. *Everyone Shampoos.* The staff is much like an ensemble. All are focused on the same thing, client service. Aria's mission is simple, "To Serve." Clients are greeted with a warm hello, something to drink, and a neck massage. There is little or no down time for clients to wait idly. And though there are *roles*, client service usurps every time. *Everyone Shampoos.* Two tier levels accommodate hair stylist stations, and Mechelle, master styler, cognitively switches her chair every few months to eliminate the perception of position power. Visit Aria's website (www.ariasalonspa.com), and the only place you will see the owner's name is in the press release section. There are weekly team meetings to share best practices and lessons learned. Don't like your hair when you get home? Well, then just come on back, and Aria will redo until you are pleased. Want to try a new stylist for whatever your reason? No problem. No one's feelings are hurt. Everyone is on the same page. Service trumps individual ego. At Aria, "Service is not a department, it is an attitude."

I have often tried to get inside Mechelle and Matthew's heads, probing to find out why they do what they do with such ease, grace, and success. Largely on instinct but coupled with learning, they have created and continue to sustain an enviable culture where everyone has his or her eye on the same goal; team play is a given; feedback is embedded; experimentation is welcomed, not punished; individuals are passionate and proud. Aria is a culture where self-interest and collaboration, structure and freedom stand side by side. Aria's is an Aesthetically Intelligent culture. An artistic culture. A place where *everyone shampoos.*

Aria embraces another key aspect of the culture of the performing arts, and that is a genuine understanding of the role of the customer in alignment. Experiences are created to engage, not entertain. Aria knows that an intentional experience is incomplete without a client and that clients vary. They recognize that service happens in the moment, so they remain mindful that "intentional" does not become mindless, rote, and impersonal. Aria is in the business of creating an experience, not a commodity.

When I began my research with theatre ensembles, I did not anticipate the extraordinary role the audience plays in alignment. The audience is a critical partner, yet it is silent and invisible until the first preview, the first time the actors and the playwright's words interact with the audience. *Do they get the story? Do they laugh or sigh at the anticipated lines? What resonates with them? What characters do they connect with? What seems to throw them off? What pleases? What disappoints?* Audience reactions during previews finalize the play's delivery. From an ensemble's point of view, previews are the final rehearsal.

Performance is indeed a conversation with the audience, however the audience must never know what it takes to pull off a great performance. The synchronization of these elements should go unnoticed by the theatre patron. Those who perform and those who experience the performance become partners in shared sensemaking, in shared alignment. Absent participation of these two parties, there can be no artistic success. Acclaimed actor Kate Burton claims, "Every great play, every great musical, every great piece of art, dance, music, photography, is a collaboration between the audience and the artist, the creator and interpreter" [8]. *Isn't this relationship, this union, at the very heart of every business's success?*

Alignment is the purest outcome of one of the greatest paradoxes of theatre, the power and striving of self-interest, which by necessity, engages to produce a whole, a kind of poetry of performance. The culture of theatre, fueled by individual engagement, is a place where self-interest and collaboration peacefully partner to achieve artistic success. This relationship makes alignment in the world of the performing arts appear natural, deeply rooted in the culture.

In contrast, alignment in most business organizations is not a natural process. It takes effort. However, given that alignment or the lack of alignment does, in fact, respectively, help or hinder organizational performance, striving for alignment should not be negotiable. Business organizations, like theatre ensembles, seek rave reviews.

As you contemplate changes to yourself and to your organization, remain mindful that you cannot change one element without considering the consequences to all of the others. In the end, an organization's success is dependent on the talent and attitude of its employees, who embrace interdependency and naturally align with organization goals, employees who have an individual stake in the ground for organizational success.

AESTHETIC INTELLIGENCE IN ACTION

*A painting is never finished, it simply
stops in interesting places.*
Paul Gardner

Two responses evolve as thematic when I introduce AeI© to any group, business member, or business student. They are curiosity and skepticism. The notion that we can reclaim the power of our senses at work and at play sparks excitement and tempts new opportunities. AeI© arouses curiosity. Without exception, the notion that business can effectively adopt aspects of the culture of the performing arts arouses skepticism.

In this section, I address both of these responses with examples and applications that speak to the two critical and ongoing business imperatives I mentioned earlier in this book.

- To cultivate an environment of connection and creativity, leading to innovation.

- To develop robust and healthy relationships in a diverse and global marketplace.

Our discussion builds on our two foundational systems, as we now move from self-awareness to building groups (teams), to creating cohesive organizations. (See Figure 5.)

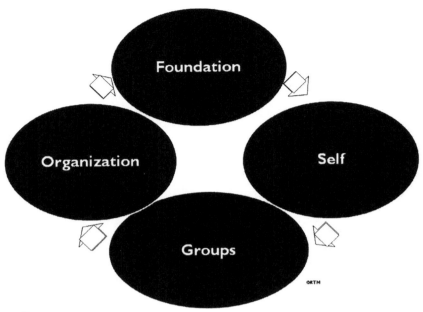

Figure 5

We begin this section with the omnipotent topic of organizational culture and explore ideas on how to create and sustain a culture of connection and creativity, which is required for innovation. Discussions on engagement and leadership follow, as they are interdependent with culture. Each chapter begins with a brief overview to establish a shared working definition. Throughout, we explore how generative conversation, the critical manifestation of AeI©, informs solutions for intrapersonal, interpersonal, and organizational challenges and opportunities. I complete this section demonstrating how and why AeI© poises people and companies to grapple with ongoing change. Examples and applications embody the full utility of the senses, demonstrating presence, authenticity, and synthesis in action.

I encourage you to heed the advice offered by one of my MBA students.

> While I may not be able to apply each lesson to an entire business, I can at minimum, change my sphere of influence, whether that is an individual application or in a

team environment or. If nothing else, the passion that I bring to my own sphere of influence is something that I can control on a daily basis.

It is easy to throw up your hands and claim that doing something different is not possible. This behavior is what management expert Jeffrey Pfeiffer speaks to in *No Excuses Leadership* [53]. Pfeiffer looks to SAS Institute as a company that does not govern by excuses. SAS is the largest privately held software company, a company that reported in 2004 twenty-eight years of revenue growth since its inception. SAS has made *Fortune's* list of the best places to work every year, enjoys an enviable 3 to 5 percent employee turnover rate, compared with an industry average of nearly 20 percent, and boasts an astounding 98 percent client subscription renewal rate [54]. SAS offers multiple examples for aspiring companies, yet ironically their story often triggers a lead by excuses response. When David Russo, a former head of Human Resources at SAS, speaks on employee loyalty and motivation, he shares that within the first 20 minutes someone in the audience raises a hand to explain that what SAS has done cannot be done in their organization. *Why bother showing up for a speech or reading a book for inspiring ideas if you are not going to try anything new?*

Excuses are rampant and easy to utter. They shut down people, connections, and ideas. "Excuses drag organizations toward failure and mediocrity," says Pfeiffer. AeI© serves to open the dialogue, invite the emergent, and allow for possibilities. It is about choice, and the choice is now yours: make excuses *why not*, or read on to discover *how*.

At the end of each section, I pose the challenge, *What will you do differently in your sphere of influence?* I offer probing questions and suggestions based on the discussed examples. So as you read, scribble in the margin and highlight items of interest. Let's compare notes (peek if you like, but the list absent context is less meaningful).

CULTIVATING A CULTURE OF CONNECTION, CREATIVITY, AND INNOVATION

And now we're progressing yet again – to a society of creators and empathizers, of pattern recognizers and meaning makers. .
Daniel Pink

Culture is an explicit and implicit force.

Edgar Schein, culture and leadership guru, defines culture as the "deeper level of basic assumptions and beliefs that are shared by members of an organization, that operate unconsciously, and that define in a basic 'taken-for-granted' fashion an organization's view of itself and its environment" [55]. Culture encompasses the collection of overt and covert rules, values, systems, and principles that guide employee behavior and practice. Cultural habits and patterns are passed on effortlessly, taught from one generation to another, dictating to members the "correct" way to perceive, think, and feel. These shared assumptions provide meaning, beget predictability, and therefore serve to reduce individual anxiety.

Informally, culture can be defined as *the way we do things around here*. Culture is organic, nurtured, and matures over time. It is a means of sensemaking.

Culture makes itself known through artifacts, values, and beliefs.

Artifacts refer to the most visible, hearable, feelable creations. These include behavior patterns (ceremonies, rituals, customs), communication patterns (language, slogans, stories, myths/metaphors, heroes, villains, anecdotes, jokes, jargons), physical attributes (dress codes, art, space design, logos, building décor), mission, vision, and goal statements.

Values are the espoused reasons for why things should be as they are represented through artifacts. They inform decision-making, conflict resolution, and communicate the way things *ought to be*, creating the blueprint for acceptable norms of behavior. Over time, values go underground, becoming unexamined and automatic thoughts. *This is how we have always done it!*

Beliefs are the implicit and unquestioned reasons that guide what group members feel, perceive, think, and act in response to external and internal issues. Beliefs show up in an organization's attitudes and approaches toward the environment, reality, time, space, human relationships and nature (commonly represented by control systems, informal language, boundary definition, rewards and punishment, status, space, and power). *Are people lazy or hardworking? Should members be proactive, reactive, or fatalistic, controlled and monitored, trusted and liberated? Does the organization reward individualism, competitiveness, or collaboration? Is conflict welcomed or avoided? Does the organization focus on the past, present or future? How easily does the organization adapt and/or integrate to new stimuli? How autocratic or democratic is the environment? Are decisions made rationally or swayed by outside moral and/or political influences?*

Leadership plays a key role in defining culture. Members watch leaders to see what they reward and measure, whom they recruit, promote, and reward. This sends a clear message to organizational members. Leaders get the behavior they tolerate. Leaders create, sustain, and/or change organizational culture, and this includes the subcultures that naturally form as units of the larger global culture.

Culture is neither good nor bad. It is subjective. Judgment cannot be made about any culture except from within it. This is the essence of what is meant by *cultural fit*. Not everyone is a good fit for the rigorous culture of GE, or the playfulness of IDEO. Objectively, neither culture is bad or good. That determination is a reflection of how well you fit, whether that specific culture is a good match for you. When individual and organizational espoused values, beliefs, and behaviors sync with the vision, objectives, and strategy, people will feel (and be) aligned and this synergy will enhance their commitment and performance. Misalignment results in serious inconsistencies, and it weakens cohesiveness and performance. A similar analogy holds true for planned change. That which runs counter to current culture will be more difficult to achieve and will likely fail without culture modification.

Several times throughout this book, I have stated that the culture of the performing arts embodies many of the cultural attributes business organizations covet. An Aesthetically Intelligent organization mirrors the culture of the world of arts, a space of possibilities where trust is given before earned, protocol is clear, competency valued, and interdependency is a constant. Whereas these coveted attributes are embedded in the culture of the performing arts, a business entity must cognitively seek to create, cultivate, and sustain them. Learning from the artist's world represents an intersection of disciplines, the nature of which is lauded in the popular text *The Medici Effect* by Frans Johansson [56]. According to Johansson, an "explosion of ideas" erupts when fields (disciplines, cultures, or other domains) intersect. These intersections are places where knowledge and practice meet. These intersections offer ideal opportunities to innovate.

Connection, creativity, and innovation cannot be mandated any more than engagement or motivation. This is one of the most prevalent myths I confront in the workplace or the classroom. The only action a leader at any level can take to facilitate these desired attitudes and behaviors is to create an environment that ignites individual intrinsic motivation, a place where engagement can thrive. By the time adults reach the workplace, their innate and uninhibited curiosity and imagination have been stifled by years of socialization and schooling. Creativity has given way to conformity. Creating an environment that rekindles this innate capacity is both a challenge and opportunity, and I suggest an imperative for leaders.

One doesn't manage creativity; one manages *for* creativity. So it seems appropriate to take a look at a few companies known for their bold innovation and sustained success. These companies have tackled the task of creating and/or transforming, and sustaining a culture of connection, creativity, and innovation. These organizations know that...

> **Individuals ➢ Energy ➢ Alignment = Collective Energy & Performance©**

What golden nuggets can you mine from their stories?

W. L. Gore, mentioned previously in our discussion on generative conversation, was named the most creative company in the United States in a 2004 *Fast Company* assessment and retains a place on their list published in 2008. As stated earlier, W. L. Gore is a privately held organization, established in 1958, which now employs over 6,300 people and sells over one thousand products. It is doubtful that founding father Bill Gore was explicitly applying AeI© to his decisions; however, his decisions embody AeI© and provide an initial platform to better understand how to intentionally embed presence, authenticity and synthesis into daily organizational life.

Geography and demographics facilitate connection and generative conversation at W.L. Gore. To recap, small, plain buildings are nestled together, each serving as home to a mix of roles and functions. Each building houses no more than two hundred people from R&D, Marketing, Sales, and Finance. Cross-functional groups congregate in simple surroundings, spawning formal and informal engagements. People comingle, and it is this convergence that causes ideas to percolate and sometimes surface, to gain traction and forge otherwise unlikely collaborations. As in the performing arts, this environment encourages people to experiment without trepidation, to be more willing to go off the straight path. As in an artistic performance, people are seamlessly working in tandem.

Gore knew that innovation is inefficient and cannot be bound by timeframes. Unlike most organizations that attempt to control innovation, Gore knew that creativity does not happen in response to time pressures or deadlines. Creativity requires an incubation period, time to allow ideas to soak and bubble up. Gore employees are not pressured to invent. For example, the elixir guitar strings were two years in the making, conceived by accident when two employees were on holiday fishing. Creativity is not due on Thursday at 3:00 p.m.

Gore strove to strengthen meaningfulness and diminish fear. Accordingly, there is minimal hierarchy and few titles at W. L. Gore. There are no bosses; rather, there is a "starting sponsor." Your team is your "boss" because like an artistic ensemble, you do not want to let the team down. You attract other talented people with your passion for what you're working on and because of the credibility you have gained over time. You become a trusted leader by leading and getting followers.

Gore wanted an organization that did not wait for a crisis to discard the rules. Accordingly, he mimicked the artist's world, dramatically altering the typical relationship between failure and risk by celebrating failure with champagne. Retooling and learning from mistakes is a routine process. At W. L. Gore, unknowing and improvisation is a welcomed way of being.

W. L. Gore has become an icon that inspires companies industry wide, and it is referenced in hundreds of articles and textbooks on creativity and innovation. You will recognize the W. L. Gore influence in the company profiles that follow.

Pixar Animation Studios has also built a culture of collective creativity and sustained innovation. Their technological and artistic breakthroughs are homegrown, created by an internal community of artists. Ed Catmull, cofounder of Pixar and president of Pixar Animation Studios and Disney Animation, credits their "adherence to a set of principles and practices for managing creative talent and risk" in their company as responsible for their success [57]. These principles stem from the cultural belief that lasting relationships matter and that "talent is rare." Striving for the best demands that Pixar is a place where it must be "safe to tell the truth." Management's role is not to "prevent risk but to build the capability to recover when failures occur." Pixar's efforts to eliminate fear resonate with what Daniel Oestreich reported in his text *Driving Fear Out of the Workplace*, that when there is fear, employees withhold information, bury the *undiscussables*, and, in turn, leave leaders uninformed. To protect their culture, Pixar leadership "constantly challenges their assumptions to surface and eliminate potential destructive flaws." They unearth *undiscussables*. Notable and impressive, Pixar bucked the norm when these principles and practices proved durable and transferable through a successful merger with Disney in 2006.

Pixar knows that creativity is not an act by one, but rather the result of complex involvement of large numbers of people from different disciplines, working together effectively to solve a range of varied problems. Success depends upon connection and creativity across levels throughout the artistic and technical parts of the organization. These actions are consistent with what Keith Sawyer, author, professor, and creativity expert, tells us in his text *Group Genius*. He writes, "Innovation always emerges from a series of sparks – never a single flash of insight" [58]. Sawyer's conclusions come from a ten-year study of jazz and improv ensembles, where he came to view these groups as the "purest forms of collaboration."

Pixar's founders were not naïve. They recognized that getting talented people is not easy and neither is getting talented people to work together. To overcome this challenge, they strove to create a robust community, a peer culture of trust and respect. A place where "talented people were loyal to one another and their collective work; a place where everyone felt that they were a part of something extraordinary and that their passion and accomplishments would make their community a magnet for talented people coming out of schools or other places" [57]. They achieved their objectives, and Pixar has become a supportive environment that fosters interdependency and, as in the arts, a place where self-interest and collaboration stand side by side. Collective creativity flourishes at Pixar.

Practice is where the rubber meets the road, where principles are embedded in everyday ways of being. For example, Pixar believes that once you get great people, you need to invest in them by giving them space, support, and feedback from everyone while at the same time preserving their creative ownership. To this end, incubation teams include directors, artists, and storyboard staff, who join to assist filmmakers in fine-tuning their ideas during the early stages of their work. These feedback sessions help new directors gain senior leadership to support their projects. This process resonates with aspects of a typical rehearsal. Blake Hall, actor and director, explains how rehearsal works. "Everyone has different ideas and taking those different ideas and making them into one big one—well, it's awesome. Especially when you start off with very different ideas and the compromise that comes with the finished product." Blake's description of a cast rehearsal also rings true for a Pixar incubation team, where ideas are freely offered and blend. Pixar leadership views incubation teams as one way to navigate uncertainty, minimize risk, and avoid mediocrity.

The Brain Trust group, composed of the top-tier directors, is another feedback resource for directors. Any director or producer can convene the Brain Trust when he or she desires advice on current projects. A two-hour open discussion follows the presentation of the work in progress. The objective is to make the film better and to avoid making errors before it is too late. The process is dependent on mutual trust and respect. Feedback is direct, apolitical, and people do not fret over being polite. Despite seniority and clout, The Brain Trust group has no decision-making authority. When finished, decision-making rests with the presenting director. The extent of the Brain Trust influence resides in the real-time process, not beyond. These guiding principles facilitate unfiltered expert opinions that enable directors at all levels to seek help in a safe environment.

The Dailies at Pixar mimic the dailies of a performing ensemble. The daily is a process for giving and getting constant feedback in a welcomed manner. On a daily basis, works in progress are made available to the entire crew, and everyone is encouraged to offer input. This process counters the normal human tendency of hoarding work until it is nearly done and it is too late to change it. Sharing consistently and early eliminates the embarrassment that often accompanies showing a rough work in progress, and this, in turn, avoids wasted efforts and opens the door to further creativity. As a bonus, it serves as a source of learning from others.

Incubation teams, the Brain Trust, and dailies work together to set people up for success by giving them the information they need to do the job well without telling them how to do it. This resonates with the culture of the arts, where experimentation is visible and audible. I am reminded of phrases I heard at rehearsals from directors—"maybe, perhaps, let's try it, we'll see"—and statements such as "there are no mistakes, only questions that will bring everyone closer to honoring their characters." Trust and feedback are as interdependent at Pixar as they are embedded in the world of the performing arts.

The physical space of Pixar is designed to forge connections and diffuse barriers and status just like at W. L. Gore. At the center of the building is a large atrium that contains the cafeteria, meeting rooms, bathrooms, and mailboxes, positioned to maximize chance encounters. This is one example of how Pixar's core and divergent disciplines of technology and art are pulled together.

At Pixar, sharing information between departments is encouraged. Employees do not need to fret over proper channels. Managers are encouraged to seek out direct reports and peers to solve problems. Managers are not expected to know all the answers. Rather, they are expected to create a safe place for everyone to offer ideas, inviting and following up with a wide range of participants.

Keeping fresh is highly valued at Pixar. Ed Catmull urges new hires to speak up when he talks with them at their welcome orientation. He sets the stage by sharing his own flaws, fumbles, and failures, and he hopes this deliberate exposure of vulnerability will ensure that newcomers understand they are beginning a learning journey where they are expected to succeed and fail. To keep ahead of the curve, Pixar encourages its employees to study and publish, to stay on top of ideas and participate in the academic community. Pixar University further provides opportunity for the department members to mingle and learn together.

These are some of the ways that Pixar defends against complacency, seeks new ideas, nurtures talent, and honors contributions to sustain an open, enviable culture of connection, creativity, and innovation.

IDEO is one of the world's leading design firms. The company employs over five hundred people, maintains eight offices on three continents, and has contributed to more than three thousand products in forty plus industries. This accomplishment has made IDEO a *go to* company for insights on creativity and innovation. In fact, it is ranked tenth in the 2008 *Fast Company* list of most innovative companies. IDEO has become the GE of the twenty-first century as business leaders try to get inside the IDEO brain, making the invisible, visible. Founder David Kelley emphasizes the power of language when he explains why he believes IDEO is so successful.

> We moved from thinking of ourselves as designers to thinking of ourselves as design thinkers ... and as design thinkers, we have a creative confidence that when given a difficult problem, we have the methodology that enables us to come up with a solution that nobody has before. [59]

With these words, IDEO became an expert at employing a methodology that enabled the company to be creative at will. It moved from a design company to a company that transforms systems.

Tim Brown, CEO and President of IDEO, offers additional insights on the characteristics of a design mindset and what it takes to create a generative design process in an organization. Brown explains that design thinkers are empathetic, keen observers and easily see the world from others' points of view. The beginning of an IDEO project begins with gaining a deep understanding of the intended audience. Design thinkers by definition are present and authentic, and they notice and absorb a broad landscape. These qualities propel them to be integrative thinkers, to move beyond analytical thinking toward novel solutions. They are synthesizers. Brown describes design thinkers as optimistic people convinced there is always a solution, folks who relish experimentation and eagerly collaborate with diverse disciplines. IDEO rejects the "lone inventor myth" and knows that innovation is born out of many, not one.

Putting process to paper, Brown maps out the design process as a "system of spaces rather than a predefined series of orderly steps" [60]. *Inspiration* begins with a problem, challenge, or opportunity introduced by the client to be explored by an interdisciplinary group. Multiple groups work simultaneously to optimize cross-fertilization and solution generation. This unrestrictive space is the place where the big ideas surface and is a unique aspect of their intentional culture. "IDEO succeeds because it has mastered improvisation," the process that dominates group work, states Keith Sawyer [58]. Like W. L. Gore employees, IDEO employees aren't assigned to teams, but they form spontaneously. Groups are kept small enough to ensure equal participation and prevent social loafing. *Ideation* expands upon selected ideas with stories and prototypes generated by the *Inspiration* space. *Implementation* moves the final solution into the marketplace.

The physical building structure and landscape align perfectly with IDEO's mission of creative competence and confidence.

Palo Alto headquarters is a "cluster of buildings that looks like a cross between a cool Montessori school and a crash pad circa 1970 [60]." Creative supplies (markers, pads, post-it notes) and inspiration (toys and games) are everywhere. This playful environment is intentional, designed to reignite the snuffed out childlike creative aptitude of its residents.

Similar to Pixar, IDEO's innovative process resembles rehearsal spaces, where a script moves from the printed page to the stage, as experiments hone in on the final agreement between characters, props, set and audience. Sarah, director, describes the process. "There is no certainty, only unpredictability, and when *amazing* happens in a room, it is magic." Regardless of entity, this dynamic can only exist in a culture of generative conversation, places where diversity, talent, trust, and a healthy respect for failure dominate. IDEO and the world of the performing arts show us they are such places. They are both living mediums.

Cisco Systems has become a symbol of business strength and resilience in an industry that enjoyed rapid, heralded growth, only to be battered in the technology bubble burst in 2001. John Chambers, CEO, can be credited with creating a firm that would stand up to the toughest times, as well as continue to forge new territory during challenging economic times. In the midst of a deep recession in 2008, Chamber embarked on a reorganization to shift the reins of power and decision-making from a small group of senior leaders to a network of global, cross-functional internal boards and councils, each unit operating like a start-up. Chambers pursued this strategy and willingly removed himself as a necessary player in many big decisions in order to ensure that Cisco would retain its enviable market share and remain a creative and innovative place to work. This year Cisco was ranked fifth by *Fast Company Magazine's* 2008 list of most innovative organizations.

The result is an evolved culture at Cisco, which focuses on people working together like never before. Leaders of business units formerly competing for power and resources now share responsibility for one another's success. This is a dramatic change from the past, from a "cowboy culture" of strong personalities, command, and control. This breed of bottom up and incremental collaboration usurps competition. Chamber deemed that the current global environment demanded such change. Today, senior leadership's compensation is based on how well collective businesses perform. Success is no longer determined by how many resources one individual controls; it is determined by how many resources an individual brings to the table. Cisco's goal is to get more products to market faster, and it is working. Internal groups are innovating with tremendous speed. A business plan that historically took six months can now be accomplished in less than one week. Cisco's culture is becoming a place where leadership and ideas come into view uninhibited by headquarters or central command. Cisco's new value and new way of being is captured by their stated vision, "Collaboration ➤ Co-Labor, means working toward a common goal." This description echoes the environments of W. L. Gore, IDEO, Pixar, and the culture of the performing arts [61].

At the core of Cisco's renewed culture is trust, collaboration, and connection, a "culture where it is unacceptable not to share what you know," says Mike Mitchell, technology director [61]. Social networking is heavily promoted by internal blogs, videos, and a Facebook- type internal communication system. These social networks invite everyone into the process, help people find resources, gather unfiltered ideas, and seek feedback. Cisco is teaching their employees to use the very products they sell and, in the process, is becoming a laboratory of connectedness and productivity. These connections dismantle internal silos and forge collaboration, becoming the mechanism of problem solving and innovation. John Chambers is quick to share that collaboration works only if it is what the CEO believes and if he or she is willing to make requisite structural changes. Cisco is a model of culture change and leadership across industry and function.

General Electric is another example of a mature and successful company that continues to evolve. CEO, Jeffrey Immelt had already achieved great success with pioneering programs such as "Ecomagination" and "Imagination Breakthroughs"; however, the decisions on these programs and their ultimate successes could be tracked back to headquarters. Immelt, echoing Chamber's motivation, knew that to accelerate organic growth he had to pass the decision-making baton to the field. In 2006, Immelt pursued an ambitious effort at General Electric to shift culture and leadership to do just that. To launch the movement, senior leaders (2,500 people in 260 teams) came together for an intensive and experiential learning program called "Leadership, Innovation, and Growth" (LIG). The objective was to have business units integrate innovation into day to day operations, to make it "as much of a religion at GE as Six Sigma had been under Jack Welch" [62]. The growth focus was on the future, to anticipate and predict opportunities. At the end of the initial four days, packed with candid straight talk and dialogue, teams submitted a growth action plan in the form of a commitment to Immelt.

The program was a catalyst for cascading changes throughout business units. Leaders examined how they spent their time. They empowered and encouraged employee involvement, identified and nurtured new talents. Simple changes had huge impact. For example, ensuring that conference calls were scheduled to include all international partners was a departure from the past when people living in an inconvenient time zone were left out of the dialogue. In the spirit of Martin's *Opposable Mind,* they departed from the historical GE conversation where you are *either* operationally excellent *or* a growth company, never both. Steven Bolze of GE Power Generation division explains, "In today's environment we can't just do one or the other" [62].

GE identified the cultural attributes of an innovative organization to which they aspired and built the LIG and its corresponding metrics accordingly[62]. Take a look at their list, and compare it to the list I offered you at the beginning of this book describing the culture of the performing arts. (See Table 3.)

General Electric Culture	Performing Arts Culture
Challenge/Involvement: members feel connected and stretched by their work and take pride in it. *Freedom:* members feel empowered to try new approaches to their work. *Trust/Openness:* members feel safe sharing ideas and working with one another. *Idea Time and Support:* members have time to think about and develop new ideas and encourage one another's ideas. *Conflict and Debate:* members experience personal tension and interpersonal warfare at work and constructively discuss and challenge one another's ideas and approaches. *Risk Taking:* members can make decisions and take action in the face of uncertainty. *Playfulness/Humor:* members see their workplace as easy going, fun, and relaxed.	*Team play* is a given, and everyone has their eye on the same prize. *Feedback* is ongoing and embedded. *Experimentation* is welcomed, not punished. **Individuals passionately and proudly** invest one hundred percent of their energy and focus every day. *Pride* and *playfulness, compromise* and *competency, self-interest* and *collaboration,* and *structure* and *freedom* stand side by side. **A world where ego, self-direction, and individuality aptly describe the players; respect, connection, and dependency, describe how they play.**

Table 3

The parallels are striking and undeniable. Indeed, the companies discussed in this chapter have created or evolved their cultures to mirror the culture of the performing arts. These organizational giants sought to be a *Yes, And* culture. They wanted to empower imagination and reconceive the words and the accompanying actions that are usually associated with failure. For these organizations, failing is a part of achieving, an essential space of learning, a critical dimension of open sharing and exploring. Jeff Bezos, founder and CEO of Amazon, shares, "You have to be willing to repeatedly fail—and to be misunderstood for long periods of time" [63]. When it comes to innovation, there is no finish line.

These are work environments where people are fully utilizing their senses, are present, authentic, and synthesize. Their culture facilitates the imagination and embraces the unpredictable. They are cohesive entities that engage their audience (customers and stakeholders) in memorable ways.

There is little doubt that a well-cast play makes for a smoother rehearsal process than one that is poorly cast. There is little doubt that when ensemble members like each other, the process feels easier. There is little doubt that when a director is collegial, trusting, and involves people, the cast is energized. There is little doubt that the presence of a diva of any kind causes a blemish on the process. However, there is no doubt that even when these desired elements are absent, the cast still rallies around the single goal, the ensemble performance. Disappointment and disagreements are not taken on stage. Renee, actor, captures this when she says, "Success ultimately depends on everyone. Everyone's job is reliant on everyone else's." I think these words stand true for any of the companies introduced in this section. Successful and innovative organizations create lasting ensembles that prosper in the best and worst of times.

Sustaining a culture of connection, creativity, and innovation is an ongoing process, and I hope these company stories have demonstrated that whether you are a start-up or well-established, cultures can evolve with leadership guidance and structural changes. In such organizations, everyone's job is connection, creativity, and innovation. *It is possible!*

WHAT WILL YOU DO DIFFERENTLY IN YOUR SPHERE OF INFLUENCE?

Cultivating a Culture of Connection, Creativity, and Innovation

- ☐ Write down your mission. *Is it one of connection, creativity and innovation?* Ask others what the mission is and see if they agree. Cultivate a habit of challenging each proposed action by asking, "Does this action serve my mission?"

- ☐ Encourage groups to employ adjunct "stakeholder" players. Not every member needs to be a full-time member. Peripheral partners enrich the dialogue.

- ☐ Take walks. Observe. Talk to people. Write down the ideas you learn and share them with your team. See how you can build and grow good ideas.

- ☐ Squelch harmful competitive practices. Ask, "What keeps us from collaborating?" Root out and remedy formal and informal policies that hinder success.

- ☐ Redesign your office space. Get a round table rather than a rectangle. Position chairs so that they are next to rather than separated by furniture.

- ☐ Enlist employee input to redesign company spaces. Create and expand common areas. Post idea bulletin boards.

- ☐ Use technology to build bridges, not walls.

- ☐ Review your formal communication vehicles. *Are employee opinions solicited? Listened to? Reacted to? Patronized? Is information shared on a need to know basis?* Remedy as demanded to maximize involvement and ownership.

- ☐ Strengthen your company orientation and town halls with straight talk and stories from leaders that speak to your culture and values. Create a huge organizational map (similar to what you find in a large museum or train station) and let everyone know where they are and how they contribute to the overall mission.

- ☐ Make it standard that anyone who attends a conference or learning event on company time comes back and shares with the team and stakeholders. This not only spreads the learning, but it ensures a return on investment.

- ☐ Adopt a max-mix seating arrangement for meeting participants to force intersections and ensure that issues will be looked at through different lenses. Max-mix means maximum mix, where each table or group assignment represents a microcosm of the organization—every level, function, and demographic.

- ☐ Bring toys to meetings. I have only one rule; they should be soft so no one can accidentally hurt anyone else. My favorite is a stretchy alien that comes in several glowing colors. Since most of my work involves learning and change, I use these aliens to make a point. When confronted with "Yes, but!" hold up your stretchy alien and proclaim, "Let the alien idea in!" When one needs to be reminded of what it takes to learn and grow, stretch the alien. "No pain, No gain!" Other neat toys include slinkies, pipe cleaners, flexible pencils, and Play-Doh. Check out Oriental Trading and similar vendors for great toy ideas.

Reframe Failure and Feedback

- ☐ Institutionalize follow-up and debriefs for meetings and conversations. *What worked? What did not work? What should be done differently and why?*

- ☐ Embrace vulnerability. Expose mistakes. People are more apt to trust you if you share good and bad news equally.

- ☐ Intentionally challenge the status quo. Invite debate. Insist that listeners challenge your ideas. Throw a curveball now and then to those folks who present to you. Force multiple ways to approach problems before settling on solutions. Delegate decision-making without punishment.

- ☐ Seek out feedback from direct reports and peers. If they are not coming to you for help, offering new or challenging ideas, and talking about the organization and its problems, then assume the environment does not allow it and find out how to fix it.

- ☐ Make organizational changes and be transparent. Eliminate titles and hierarchy that get in the way of generative conversation.

Embed a Rehearsal Mindset

- ☐ Test out ideas and presentations with peers. Create the equivalent of an incubation team, Brain Trust, and dailies.

- ☐ Run through your "presentation" and see if it makes sense, tells a good story, and has clear segues. Do not lose sight of the fact that you are indeed performing each time you step in front of colleagues.

- ☐ Eliminate time constraints on so-called innovation work.

- ☐ Write in pencil.

Cultivate Improvisation

- ☐ Pay attention to what your senses are telling you, and act on that information. Do not leave a meeting talking to yourself. Rather capture in real time… *What ticks you off? What ignites your energy?* Encourage others to engage in similar self-probing. Reflect, share, and utilize this information to strengthen individual and interpersonal relationships.

- Write a paragraph on what areas you have identified in yourself that need "improvisational" improvement. Think about interactions where you wish you had said or done something differently.

- Mimic, the "Yes, And" activity to stimulate idea exploration.

- Track your responses to conversations. *Are you a "Yes, And" or a "Yes, But" person?*

- Collect copies of cartoons similar to the ones made famous in the *New Yorker* or the *Sunday Parade* magazine. Cut off the given captions and pass them out to a group. Have folks create their own captions. Enjoy the diversity. Expand the possibilities. Emphasize how different people see the very same thing differently.

- Use storytelling to play with ideas and review events. Imagine how things could be or have to be different. Here are a few versions of activities that build on opening story lines, which are introduced in Daniel Pink's book *A Whole New Mind*.

Example: Pick up a text or magazine and randomly underline one sentence. Build a story based on that one-liner.

Example: Visit your favorite bookstore or library and select several magazines that you do not normally read, ones in which you have no interest. Then peruse them in search of connections to your life and work. You will be surprised to see where you find inspiration and ideas that you can *steal shamelessly.*

Example: Ask everyone in a given group to write one opening line on an index card (for example, "When I walk into our reception area…"). Place all the index cards in a hat or container, and then, taking turns, have each person draw a card and tell a story on the spot that begins with the line on the card. You can focus this activity by applying this to a particular product, service, or experience. See what big ideas crop up and what themes surface.

Example: Create a list of story line openers. Customize the list to fit the situation you are exploring. Place one story line on the top of each participant handout. Organize people into small groups of four to seven. Distribute one story line paper to each participant, and ensure that each group member has a different story line opener. Instruct participants to read the story line on their paper and write the next sentence that seems to flow from the first. Encourage free association and spontaneity, and remind participants that there are no wrong second sentences. When everyone has completed composing one sentence, ask participants to pass the papers to the person on their right. Repeat the process so that each person then reads two sentences and adds a third. Continue passing along story lines until everyone's original paper has circulated twice around the group (for instance, in a five-person group, each story would be ten lines long). Ask each person to read the story on their paper to their group. Follow with a group discussion of the situation. Have each group share its best ideas or insights with the larger group. Help the group recognize the ease and difficulty of adding a story line, the constraints of judgment, the challenge of keeping an open mind, and the value of the process in generating original thinking. Sample story line openers include:

1. The first thing I noticed when I walked into our office building...
2. The people I work with are usually...
3. Clients seem to be...
4. Challenges at work...
5. My wish list for next year would...
6. If I have difficulty making a decision, I think of...
7. I knew I should...
8. No one told me that...
9. Before you know it, the meeting...
10. We always begin...
11. I would be hard-pressed to share...
12. People seem hesitant to...
13. I am confident that leadership...
14. If I could change one thing about my job...
15. It's understood that...

What additional ideas would you add to this list?

ENGAGEMENT: PEOPLE POWER

You can dream, create, design, and build the most wonderful idea in the world, but it requires people to make the dream a reality.
Walt Disney

Organizations of all kinds consist of individuals with energy to expend. Culture defines the environment, how people think and behave. Alignment of individuals to their representative culture strengthens engagement and optimizes energy. The relationship of these aspects determines performance.

> **Individuals ➢ Energy ➢ Alignment = Collective Energy & Performance©**

The world of the performing arts is abundant with individual energy. It is visible and audible. It is inspiring and contagious. This palpable energy draws from an artist's deep intrinsic engagement and is observable as ensembles rally around the common goal of performance. Here again, business leaders can be inspired by lessons from the culture of the performing arts, a culture whose underpinning is AeI©.

Employee engagement refers to the people who work at the intersection of maximum role satisfaction and maximum role contribution. Employee engagement is where knowledge, energy, and passion meet. Engaged employees carve out and remain in their *Sweet Spot:* a role they enjoy, are good at, and is valued by the organization[64]. (See Figure 6.) Engaged employees are proud, know how their work contributes to overall goals and objectives, believe their employers care, feel a profound connection to their company, produce more, stay longer, and therefore, nurture profit. The *Sweet Spot* resonates with how author Tim Rutledge describes engaged employees in his text *Getting Engaged: The New Workplace Loyalty*. He writes, "Engaged employees are attracted to, and inspired by their work ("I want to do this"), committed ("I am dedicated to the success of what I am doing"), and fascinated ("I love what I am doing") [65]. Although Rutledge is describing employees, his words capture the profile of a performing artist or any other individual who loves his or her work. Engagement is a place of congruency between self and the whole.

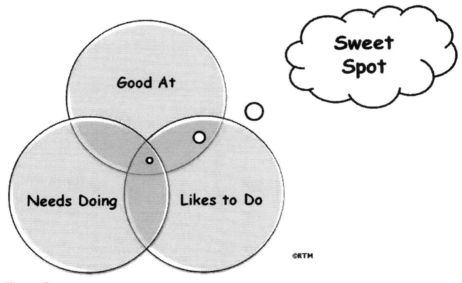

Figure 6

Organizational energy, engagement, is the fuel, the propelling force with which a company functions. This brand of collective engagement is an attitude nurtured by individuals who are intrinsically motivated, self-determined, moving enthusiastically in the same direction and exerting their discretionary effort to help their company succeed.

At this point, you may be grumbling to yourself, saying things my clients and students often say such as "it's not possible to live and work your passion," or you may be thinking similar statements that suggest *love* and *work* do not go together. Artists love their work, but they do not hold exclusive rights on being able to say, "I can't believe they pay me to do this." I am happy to say that often I leave a client or classroom and cannot believe they actually pay me to do the work I love. It is a sad commentary that socialization sanctions it is okay to compromise our passions and become a commodity, a byproduct of snuffing out innate creativity, imagination, and the full utility of our senses.

The companies profiled in the previous chapter courageously made other choices and worked hard to create Aesthetically Intelligent environments that cultivate engaged employees and encourage people to thrive in their Sweet Spots. Their employees are similar to the artists I met in my fieldwork. Their stories exude passion and fulfillment, and like artists, their fulfillment is not derived from financial incentives, but rather from doing work they love and loving the people with whom they work. Consider that at any given time, only 20 percent of equity actors are actually getting paid for work, and most actors earn considerably less than twenty thousand dollars a year. Though I am not advocating a compensation revolution for the business lexicon, I think this fact emphasizes that money does not engage or motivate people. Money is not and never will be a substitute for intrinsic drive. Indeed, I sensed an almost superior attitude from the artists with whom I met regarding the financial disparity between the arts and business. I call this the *Happy Factor*. Artists are aware of the choices they make, and they have chosen to be happy with work as opposed to being indifferent to or dreading it, words they hear frequently from business brethren who took the more conventional route. They are elated to be a part of a process that is always thrilling—from audition to opening night. I find this enviable, worth striving for.

If an organization aspires to be an industry leader, to be best in class, then achieving employee engagement must not be viewed as something that would be nice to have; it should be a necessity. Employee engagement defines the bottom line. It is not a small deal. Consider that *The Gallup Organization* reports the price tag for employees who are actively or moderately disengaged is projected to cost the U.S. economy about $370 billion annually [66]. They estimate a mere 15 percent of employees are actively engaged in their jobs, who, like performing artists, are self-directed, and work with passion and energy [67]. An astounding near 30 percent of employees are actively disengaged. They spend their company paid time pursuing other jobs, rousing peers, and causing disruption. The remaining 55 percent or so are moderately disengaged, sleepwalking through their workday, putting time, not passion, into their work. They are misaligned and alienated from the company and the work. These employees are benchwarmers, lost opportunities.

I could toss more statistics at you, but I do not have to. You do not need to be a mathematician to calculate employee disengagement leaves a lot of money on the table. Disengagement negatively affects customer service, employee morale, attendance, retention, company credibility, and shareholder value. Disengagement exacerbates absenteeism and turnover. You know this because you are a customer. You are a shareholder. You know this because disengaged employees make themselves known. They are easy to see and hear. Their detachment lingers and influences where you shop, dine, and vacation.

So what can you do? I addressed part of this question previously when we explored self-awareness and our stories. This type of personal work will help you, as individual discover your *Sweet Spot*. Then it will be up to you to go live it.

As an organizational leader, you can strive to create an environment that invites and sustains engagement. By now, I hope you accept that engagement cannot be demanded, dictated, or bought and that financial incentives pale miserably compared to the intrinsic factors of passion, competency, enjoyment, and meaningfulness. Given the stark differences in engagement data between the world of business and the world of the arts, I suggest there is much to learn from the performing arts. Actor, director, and musician David de Vries explains:

> In a theatre company, you are your human resources. That is all - it is up on the stage. If you do not value that, appreciate what each individual actor brings to a role, you have nothing. Corporate cultures could learn to apply that same kind of wisdom to their approach.

Unfortunately, the platitude, "people are our most valuable asset," is often more rhetoric than action. However, some companies, including those mentioned in the culture section, recognize that engaged people are their most valuable asset and have taken strategic actions to ensure they buck the trend. SAS is a stunning example. They have designed a culture that revolves around employee engagement, and like the world of the arts, this culture optimizes employees' discretionary effort. Since developers at SAS thrive on intellectual stimulation, SAS generously sends them to industry and technology specific conferences, knowing that they will return energized to share their learnings with colleagues. SAS conducts extensive employee surveys to identify and eliminate distractions which otherwise would hamper productivity. Work/Life balance is supported by an onsite medical facility, day care, basketball court, swimming pool, and gym. A corporate concierge helps employees manage daily necessities such as car wash, haircut appointments, and dry cleaning. Children are encouraged to join parents at mealtime in the corporate cafeteria. Employees have flexible start and end schedules to accommodate personal lives and are granted extra days off to attend school functions.

Work life at SAS fosters an Esprit de Corps, a devotion to the company and its purposes, a place where individual and group goals align. All this costs quite a bit of money, and hence it is not surprising that the majority of organizations do not attempt to replicate SAS. Yet, when you run the numbers, SAS saves 85 million dollars a year in recruitment of new employees because of employee retention. This number does not even include the ROI (Return on Investment) gained by internal employee promotion and accumulated intellectual capital. SAS is truly a corporate ecosystem where creativity and productivity flourish, profitability and flexibility go hand in hand, and where love, hard work, and work/life balance are not mutually exclusive.

Those in the arts and companies like SAS, Cisco, IDEO, Pixar, and W. L. Gore recognize that engagement is *intrinsically* driven, and accordingly, they have built supportive cultures and talent management systems. Based on my experience, it is baffling that most organizations appear unable to grasp this fact as evidenced by the ongoing investment in performance management systems that are largely *extrinsically* motivated. This is an act of ignorance or denial. There are other options.

Organizations can begin by assessing their culture and standardized policies and procedures to determine what is helping and hindering their quest for fully engaged employees. Once the culprits are identified, the next step is to determine what can be changed. Without the willingness to make requisite system changes, organizational rhetoric about employee engagement and talent fall flat and are prey to becoming a trend, a flavor of the month. This is a critical leadership fork in the road, a decision-making time that determines whether rhetoric, appetite, and wallet will align. It is a time of *walking the talk*. Exploring and changing antiquated systems is not for the faint-hearted; it requires courage. However, companies committed to engaging employees in their respective Sweet Spots will reap the rewards of a talented cast.

In addition to assessment, an organization needs to clearly identify what work needs to get done and what talent the organization needs to accomplish the work. These behavioral anchors translate into job titles and recruitment strategy. People are sought after because of their demonstrated or potential talent, not just their pedigree or alumni connections. Interviews for external or internal candidates are real, rigorous, and consistent. Interviews focus on inquiry and exploring the fit between person, role and company. Too often these job interviews can sound like a company sales job.

Recruitment and selection are essential organizational processes that parallel audition and casting for any given artistic performance. The directors with whom I met were quick to say that 80 percent of artistic success in theatre resides in casting. If you cast the wrong people, even a great director and script could be doomed; but if a bad director casts the right people, they might even make him or her look like a genius. I think this holds true for other ensemble performances. In the same way, a robust and effective recruitment and selection process is 80 percent of the work in achieving employee engagement, getting the *right* person, in the *right* job with the *right* company fit. Zappos, a rising online retailer offers new employees two thousand dollars to quit after their initial four-week paid training programs if they prove a poor fit. CEO and founder Tony Hsieh explains it is best to know early if an employee doesn't fit or buy into the vision and culture. "It just makes economic sense," Hsieh claims [63]. Success on Broadway and Main Street depends upon the engagement and alignment of individual players.

Actors begin their entry process with a small role. If they prove competent and develop range, bigger roles await them, and with that, actors make more money. Audition is required of everyone. Casting is most often earned by merit, by talent, and by fit. This flies in the face of how politics drives the recruitment and promotion process in many business organizations.

In the theatre, an actor does not have to become a director, producer, or set designer. Growing as a great actor, staying where they are passionate is fine. In contrast, people join organizations in entry roles where they bring the requisite talent, and ironically, when they begin to excel at their work, they are frequently forced to move up and out of that work if they want to earn more or increase their span of influence. They need to become managers of people, whether they are good at it or not, because their compensation and power are determined by their number of direct reports. When I ask aspiring managers why they want to be promoted to manager, I am most often told the decision is based on salary and clout, not a passion to develop or lead people.

When you take a person out of their Sweet Spot, you immediately suboptimize his or her talent. This action erodes individual meaningfulness, engagement, and ultimately performance. Many people may be fantastic, talented individual contributors, but they make for lousy managers. In the same vein, some great people managers are not and should not be forced to be subject matter experts. Few companies have equal tracks for individual contributors and people managers. *Can you imagine an organizational system that actually recruits and grooms great managers, great people developers?* For all the talk on the importance of developing people, organizations that make this distinction and allow for multiple career paths, each with similar financial and influence opportunities, are rare. The traditional structure offers the majority of organizational members few choices: climb the corporate ladder, linger in unfulfilling roles, or leave the organization. In all cases, engagement and therefore performance are compromised.

Once selected, onboarding processes facilitate engagement with new or promoted employees. I am not talking about inundating folks with human resource forms and policies and calling it orientation. I am talking about creating substantive initiatives that ensure employees get the professional and social guidance demanded during transition. Mentors, buddies, cross-functional exposure, colleague introductions, planned lunches, daily feedback, and conversations can all work to keep individuals, groups, and organizations aligned and energized.

Key processes such as recruitment, selection, promotion, and rewards should align individual talents and organizational needs. They should not conform to artificial organizational charts and ladders. The current incestuous path of career and compensation dooms organizations to fail in developing and retaining talent and maintaining an engaged employee population. Lip service will not cut it. The most impressive and expensive programs in leadership development will not make a difference until organizations are willing to reinvent or at least modify outdated performance management systems. Changing these outdated systems is another step toward tapping the potential of collective energy.

These are a few of the ways organizations can grow and sustain a culture of engagement. I urge organizations to get off the soapbox and to stop trying to implant or cajole employee engagement. Instead, enact structures, policies, and processes that accept engagement is largely intrinsic, self-directed, and highly emotive. It may be easier for a start-up enterprise to create a stronger engagement and talent infrastructure than it would be for a more established business; however, we have seen how giants like GE and Cisco continue to evolve. What they know is that failing to act at all is certain to ensure compromised results.

My study unequivocally concluded that people doing something they love, are good at, and is valued by the larger enterprise fosters team play, collaboration, trust, feedback, passion, playfulness, competency, creativity and experimentation. I am not so bold to state that this is new information, but I do suggest that what I have learned about the inner workings of theatre and the performing arts offers new ways of thinking about needed changes. Successful business performance relies on capturing the hearts and minds of employees, and organizations would be wise not to ignore the fact that over 50 percent of their workforce is a neutral body in a chair.

In the end, an organization's sustained prosperity is dependent on the engagement, talent, and attitude of its employees, who embrace interdependency, align with organization goals, and have an individual stake in the ground for organizational success. Employee engagement holds the promise of the ultimate prize for employers today. I believe that creating a culture that bolsters engagement and unleashes employees' potential is a choice for every business leader and organization.

From the start, my premise has been that performing arts culture embodies the attributes business organizations crave. For me, the underpinning of that culture is AeI©, defined by *Presence*, *Authenticity* and *Synthesis*. These elements reignite the full utility of our senses, and we can cultivate them individually as well as embed them into our company cultures. When translated into systems and processes, AeI© promotes the connection, creativity, and innovation across organizations essential in today's global environment. Since people comprise the energy that moves organizations, it is not possible to realize and sustain outstanding performance without engaged employees.

Whether in business or the arts, it takes great leadership to achieve great performances. We will explore what it takes to be a leader who can pull this all together in the next section.

WHAT WILL YOU DO DIFFERENTLY IN YOUR SPHERE OF INFLUENCE?

Engagement: People Power

- ☐ Determine if you are in your Sweet Spot. *Do you love what you do? Are you good at it? Does your organization appreciate your contribution?*

- ☐ Take a good look at your critical people processes. *How are people recruited? Selected? Onboarded? Recognized? Promoted?* Align! Align! Align!

- ☐ Try this icebreaker at a meeting. Ask folks to tell you their contribution to the organization, not their job title. Common sense indicates this should be a no brainer. However, most times I get rolling eyes as people struggle for the distinction. If it is hard to identify, revisit job tasks. Ensure employees' work and time is value-added and that they know what their contribution is to the greater organization.

- ☐ Ensure your direct reports are clear on expectations and tasks, and that they have the resources they need to do their work.

- ☐ Approach your manager and schedule regular conversations that are not contingent on a special project or need. Cultivate a relationship and share feedback. Talk about what is working well and not so well, and figure out how to make everything work better. Build trust, and enroll your manager to assist you in carving out your ideal career path. If you are a manager, then schedule these with your direct reports as well. Do not assume that people know what you want or that you know what others want. Find out and then respond.

- ☐ Survey less, act more. Connect! Connect! Connect!

- ☐ Observe with all your senses. Take walks. Sit in the reception area of your office. *What pulls you? What sounds resonate with you? What surroundings attract you? Do you feel energy or apathy? Are people engaged or keeping busy? How do people interact informally? Do different functions and levels interact often and easily?*

- ☐ Identify sources and actions relating to organizational motivation. *Are you and/or your company a carrot and stick mindset, or is motivation understood as intrinsic?*

- ☐ Surface, rather than avoid conflicts. Listen, empathize, and resolve, but do not undercut.

- ☐ Reflect on what recognition you crave. *Are you getting it? If not, how can you change that? Do you know what kind of recognition your direct reports crave?* If not, find out. Recognize! Recognize! Recognize!

- ☐ Create a substantive integration program for new or promoted employees. Assign a Buddy for the first three months. Lay out a three-month schedule that includes lunch plans, as well as visits to cross-functional team meetings and introductions to management. Grow and challenge people early by arranging a mentor to pick up when the Buddy's time is up.

❐ Challenge your individual need to be popular. Although it is an extra perk when you like people at work and they like you, it is not essential. Your role at work is not a popularity contest. What is essential is that your group works effectively. The goal at work is to figure out how best to work together. *What can you do differently to create this synergy?*

What additional ideas would you add to this list?

THE LANGUAGE OF LEADERSHIP

It's not about getting ahead – it's about making a difference, knowing the strengths and weaknesses of yourself and your team, and expanding your organizations' capacity to do well. That is the make of a true leader.
Michael Useem, Professor of Management, Wharton, University of Pennsylvania

Leader as a noun, is a sought after position by men and women of all ages, shapes, shades, and sizes. Lead as a verb suggest actions such as prompt, engage, enroll, energize, influence, spearhead, safeguard, and recognize. Leadership as an adjective denotes a capacity to govern. These are the dimensions of the *Language* of *Leadership*.

Organizations of all types invest millions of dollars annually to buy, build, educate, and grow leadership. In my role, I have had the pleasure of partnering with companies to help them define their leadership strategy, models, and programs. Sometimes, I kick off a meeting with the following activity. I ask the participants to name one word that comes to mind when they think of leadership, and the word must begin with the letter **L**. At first, the task seems challenging, perhaps odd, but after a few moments, the words just keep coming.

> Language, Listen, Learn, Lesson, Liberate, Leverage, Liaison, Legacy, Laughter, Laconic, Labor, Look, Launch, Legwork, Lend, Lift, Lather, Leaven, Lubricate, Link, Linkage, Loop, Limitation, Lean, Locate, Latent, Locus, Loose, Limbo, License, Lineage, Legend, Landmark, Love, Lively, Living, Labyrinth, Lacking, Large, Lark, Last, Layout, Lead, Lame, Lenient, Level, Light, Like, Loaded, Lofty, Logical, Lucrative, Loyal, Lyrical, Lordly, Low, Lonely, Long, Luck, Lull, Lucid

When the lists are completed, everyone can begin to see the *Language* of *Leadership*. The disparate words fall into self-evident categories, exposing the breadth and range of leadership attributes. To mobilize thinking and energy I highlight some key terms and pose a few reflective questions.

Language: Do you speak the language of leadership or hierarchy? Do people work *with* you or *under* you? Are you a boss or a manager? Do you have subordinates or direct reports? Do you reside in an office space that separates you or makes you a part of your group? Does your tone communicate collaboration and connection or power and control?

Listening *(laconic)*: Do you seek to understand others? Do you seek feedback and input? Think of listening in this way: *What word do you get when you rearrange the letters in LISTEN?* The answer is *SILENT,* and it speaks volumes.

Learn *(labor, look, legwork, launch, lend)*: How do you expand what you already know? Do you seek out others' experience? Do you surround yourself with people smarter than yourself? Do you know what you don't know? Do you feel like you have to have the answers? Do you know the right questions to ask?

Lesson *(latent, locate, limitation, lean, locus)*: Do you teach what you know? Do you share or hoard information? Are you constantly learning?

Liberate *(limbo, loose, license)*: Do you enable and empower those around you? Do you ensure the success of those around you? Do you credit those who do the work with the glory? Do you reward risk taking? Do you punish mistakes?

Leverage *(lather, lubricate, lift, leaven)*: Do you know your own and others' talent? Are these talents optimized? Are talents aligned well with work responsibilities? What actions do you specifically take to buoy up the talent of those with whom you work?

Liaison *(linkage, link, loop)*: With whom do you connect? Do you intentionally prepare for your various stakeholders and interactions? Do you empathize or manipulate? Do you know how to deliver your message so that diverse audiences can hear it?

Legacy *(lineage, landmark, legend)*: Are you building something to last, or are you focused on your next job, promotion, or paycheck?

Laughter *(lively)*: Do you create an environment of ease, fun, and playfulness?

Love *(like, loyal, living)*: Do you love your work?

After debriefing, the stage is set, and the group is ready to move on. Now, so are you. Although there are perhaps thousands of texts on leadership and many espoused models, leadership remains a vast concept offering diverse definitions. Still, the **L** activity demonstrates how certain themes consistently surface. The ideal leader is multidimensional, a cultural force. Leadership is an act of co-creation. Bad leadership is awful. Regrettably, too many leaders are in it for themselves—their package and their future. As I write this book, the entire global community is experiencing the worst economic downturn in a century, which has resulted from bad leaders. Wall Street and Main Street are littered with their debris.

My purpose in this chapter is twofold: to zero in on those leadership dimensions that reflect AeI© and are critical to creating, aligning, and sustaining a culture of connection, creativity, and innovation populated by engaged employees; and to discuss what leaders can learn from leaders in the world of performing arts. I have been conducting the **L** word activity for decades, but it was not until AeI© was born that I realized the characteristics and behavior that emanate rely heavily on the elements of AeI©, presence, authenticity, and synthesis, and can best be in actualized in an Aesthetically Intelligent culture of connection, creativity, and innovation.

The intersection of business and the arts is strengthened by a shared sense of what makes for leadership. Leadership is critical to both communities. A leader who enlists the collective wisdom and combined energy of individuals will outperform one who hinges solely on his or her own powers. A leader who facilitates harmony among members of an organization will see unprecedented levels of productivity. In an organization, leadership is answered with a CEO and Senior Management Team. In the arts, and specifically in theatre, a producer and director originate and drive the drama, script, cast, and crew. The director is dominant from audition to opening night; the producer ultimately has the final word if there is disagreement.

My focus here is on the director, the primary individual bearing the greatest influence on the culture and engagement of any given ensemble. The director transforms the script into an operational reality, coordinating all activities while securing the producer's approval of decisions at key junctures. He or she conducts auditions (recruitment), casts the actors (selection), creates schedules, and ensures timelines are met (project management). The director guides the selection of appropriate costumes and props (supports resources, tools, and methods), determines day-to-day movements (management), schedules and prepares rehearsals (practice, educate, coach) and more. The director does all this till opening night when the entire production is turned over to the trustful hands of the stage manager. As a layman, I never knew of such a handoff. I assumed the director stayed with the life of the show. Instead, the director is grooming the stage manager all along, preparing to pass the baton on opening night. It appears directors and business leaders share a similar menu of tasks and challenges.

First-rate directors are present. They are in the moment watching, listening, and expressing what is happening before them. Director Mira Hirsch says that a "great director collects what they (actors) are bringing." Susan Booth, Artistic Director of the Alliance Theatre, explains, "A director prepares for the conversation with the audience, harvests all the voices in the room, knows how to stand behind the cast and audience and not between." David de Vries, director, actor, and musician, shares, "You want to do everything within your power so that their performance is fully realized. The buck stops with you. Your name is on it."

As we learned, directors claim the most important thing they do is cast the play. After casting, a director recognizes that different actors need different things from them, and adapts their interactions and guidance accordingly. Sarah, director, told me she judges what an actor will need from her. "They're always going to be some weaker links. It (leading) is a juggling act which changes on any given show." A good director clearly states expectations and balances his or her need for control with empowerment. Also, a good director should know when to get involved and when to retreat. They work constructively with staff and bring conviction as well as compromise to identify and resolve issues. They accept ever present financial constraints, know what can and cannot be done, and understand that there is no one way to accomplish the tasks. He or she is the eyes and ears of the group, representing their interests with others backstage. The success of directors is determined by their ability to coordinate these multiple players and create a cohesive performance. Authenticity becomes apparent as directors get in character for each person, message, situation, and time.

Without question, the director is responsible for pulling it all together. He or she is a synthesizer, sensemaker, and sculptor, someone who notices emergent patterns from the collective process. The finest create a work environment where everybody gets to talk and everybody's ideas are honored and considered. Sarah shares:

> I don't want to dominate the conversation. What is most important to me is that at the end of the meeting everyone has had something to say. To me it is not a successful show, if somebody walks away and they were miserable.

Directors perfect a rare fusion of collaboration. They trust the talent around them and give actors space to explore and own their characters. A rehearsal is an exploration, not an exam. Mistakes are a given. Lee Devin, author and director, offers a director's view of mistakes. He says, "No one calls the second step in a staircase a mistake or failure. It doesn't get you to the top, but it is a step along the way" [6]. Reframing how we think about mistakes prompts co-creation, in-the-moment experiments, real time synthesis and decision-making.

Regardless of the director and ensemble I observed during my research, I heard encouraging phrases. "Go with your intuition." "What do you think?" "How does that feel?" "Take your time; we are doing fine." I saw and heard gestures of support: reassuring nods, warm smiles, gutful laughter, tender hugs, and pats on shoulders. Irrespective of director's different styles, I heard daily and explicit appreciation. "This is great." "Fabulous." "Wonderful." "I love it." When an actor was tackling a difficult scene, I would hear, "Are you okay?" "My heart goes out to you." "I empathize." Every day ended with "Thank you." Leadership is a relationship. The language of leadership is a dialogue, not a monologue.

The words and phrases used to describe the role and behavior of an effective director are exactly the same ones we would use to describe an ideal business leader. Like a director, he or she is a teacher, assembler, and enabler. A leader empowers people to their highest level by offering them opportunities, not obligations. Like directors, leaders put in motion a *casting* and *harvesting* process, integrated and targeted to glean the optimal performance of the individuals for the whole, the performance, the organization. These ways of being are embedded in the culture of the arts; therefore, by definition, a good director creates and sustains an Aesthetically Intelligent environment. This fact raises the classic dilemma of the chicken and the egg—or in this case, "Which comes first, the culture or the leader?" The culture of the arts has remained the same for centuries; ergo directors are products of that culture. In business, leaders are continuously mucking around with organizational culture, rendering this question more difficult to answer. Whatever the answer, it is my view that directors serve as a source of insight and inspiration for great leadership in any venue.

Most directors were actors first, and, consequently, the way directors behave stems from their strong, abiding respect and empathy for actors. Most want to be an actor's director. Listen to what actors and crew (tech staff) told me they want and/or need from a director. Their words testify to how in sync their relationship is.

Chris says, "Their (directors') job is the big picture, getting everybody pulling in the same direction, really caring about what they are doing, really doing their best and being prepared." He wants a director who appreciates that "with this group of people I can make something greater than I can alone." David recalls his best experiences were with directors who were "amazing, intelligent, quick, and funny." Isaac wants a director "who trusts the script" and knows "when to get involved and when to stand back." Joe asserts, "A smart director hires the right people for their jobs and then lets them go do their jobs. He sculpts it together." Renee summarizes:

> They are coming in to collaborate with individual artists, to organize, not run something. They are in charge of the rehearsal atmosphere. They get to make choices about timing, transition, light and dark, entrances and exits. The director sets up the dominoes, but what they don't get to do is tell me which dominoes I am going to walk through or hit. There may be a time when that happens, but if the director tries to micromanage that is not good.

Renee highlights a recurring sentiment from actors; they prefer a director who gives them room to do their craft. Neal hopes a director will "start out and give me a lot of space. Some people want and need early guidance, and I do not. I hope the director will look at my choices before they give me theirs." David says a good director "can talk to an actor and get them to do what she (or he) wants, get from them what she (or he) is looking for without saying it." Chris adds:

> I don't like (a director) telling me what do. That is bad. You get the performing *monkey feel* then. A lot of it has to do with honoring your ideas. Paying attention to what you are doing. This is the collaborative nature of it. That is why you bother having a director. We could all wind up with something alone. It is the notion that our ideas will go further than just one person's ideas.

Famed actor Martha Plimpton's writes:

> I've worked with some great directors who really knew what they were doing, were really in love with the form,

and imbued the entire atmosphere with joy and comfort and pleasure by making the work not just fun but also enriching and thoughtful. I want a director to infect everyone in the room with a joyous enthusiasm for their vision. And I want them to be able to sort of plant the seed of their idea in everyone and then help that seed to grow and flourish in the individual actor at their own pace.[8]

Actors want guidance, not directives. They want challenges, not judgments. At the same time, they expect the director to see things that others do not, to interlace the many facets and contributions into a greater whole. They trust the director to do that. Collaboration is pivotal to mutual success. These needs and wants echo the needs and wants of employees in every playing field.

What we see here is a harmonious and reflective process of shared needs and wants translated into distinct ways of being and interacting. Most senior leaders were at one time in an entry-level position. Leaders at all levels started somewhere first. *What if you executed this process at your place of work, asking your direct reports what they want from you, channeling your behavior to demonstrate your strong, abiding respect and empathy for those you work with?* Imagine the possibilities!

What becomes visible is a snapshot of how an *Aesthetically Intelligent* leader behaves and is experienced. He or she:

Present ... is in the moment, passionate, engaged and engaging, creative, vulnerable, accessible, inclusive—one who listens, observes, expresses, experiments, honors ideas, harvests voices and talent.

Authentic ... collaborates, facilitates, enables, respects, coaches, guides, trusts, empowers, knows boundaries, serves as a liaison, and prepares for a range of interactions with intention.

Synthesizer ... is a sensemaker and sculptor who absorbs, pulls together, assembles, compromises, notices patterns, and knows that greatness is an accomplishment of the whole, not an individual voice.

The value of these capacities is universal and applicable across level, function, and industry. There are two additional dimensions of AeI© leadership, *passion* and *language,* that I feel are worthy of further discussion.

Presence is bolstered by passion because passion is an emotion and a catalyst to action. Artists are passionate. Passion is visible, audible, and consistent amongst its players. However, passion is not exclusive to a few. Max Howard, actor and professional speaker, explains:

> We all have and act on passion. When you strike someone in anger that is an act of passion. When you embrace someone in kindness that is an act of passion. To live a passionate life is to feel something so powerfully that you must act on that feeling. Passion can release positive or negative energy. You may be a peacemaker, a healer, a bully, or a thief. But you must act.

Passion in action is Bill Gore (W. L. Gore), Ed Catmull (Pixar), John Chambers (Cisco), Tim Brown (IDEO) and Jim Goodnight (SAS), leaders of companies we have discussed. Passion defines Steven Jobs (Apple), Bill Gates (Microsoft), Andy Grove (Intel), Michael Dell (Dell Corp.), Jeff Bezos (Amazon) and a host of other companies we have not discussed. We have participated in passion that has moved people and changed history with Barack Obama, Nelson Mandela, Ghandi, John F. Kennedy, Martin Luther King, and similar leaders who have showed us how passion engages, compels, and mobilizes. This is what leaders do. They create a felt presence that is contagious, which causes others to listen, enroll, and expend their own energy. They move people.

Passionate leaders are experienced as authentic. The look on their faces. The tone of their voice. The words that they say. Passion is emotion. Passion is heart. Passionate leaders strive to see the world through others' eyes, acknowledge and address legitimate concerns, educate, and raise the self-esteem of those around them. Warren Bennis, leadership expert and author, declares, "Leaders love what they do and love doing it" [68]. Jack Welch, concludes:

> Passion is a heartfelt, deep, an authentic excitement about work. People with passion care—really care in their bones—about colleagues, employees, and friends winning. They love to learn and grow, and they get a huge kick when the people around them do the same. [69]

Passionate leaders deliver and encourage the best performances every day. Despite our inherent bias to dismiss emotion at work, it seems as if love and work do go together.

This chapter is titled, "Language of Leadership," because our choice of language reveals who we are and how we think, and it sets the tone for how we are with others and relates to how we listen. I have some "hot button" words, which when uttered, elicit an immediate response from me. For example, he or she works "under me" or "for me." My "boss." My "subordinate." *What is the picture you see when someone is working "under" you?* I see a bug, an insect, ripe to be smashed. I get a completely different vision when I hear "someone works *with* me." I see collaboration. The Aesthetically Intelligent leader employs collaborative, not hierarchical vocabulary, chooses language of inquiry, not advocacy. The Aesthetically Intelligent leader is a master of generative conversation.

Language and listening go hand and hand. Directors and actors are astute listeners. They need to be. Onstage there is constant communication, and an actor must stay in character and remain connected with his or her fellow actors. Blake simply states, "You can't act if you don't listen." Performing is reliant on others. Failing to listen threatens the authenticity of the performance and leads to failing one's peers. Listening at this level and intensity demands presence.

Regardless of level or location, leaders must listen too. Noel Tichy declares that "strong leaders must learn to be listening leaders" [39]. Ronald Heifetz states that "good listening is fueled by curiosity and empathy" [70]. Peter Drucker claims there is one rule for leaders: "listen first, speak last." He adds, "The leader of the past was a person who knew how to tell, the leader of the future will be a person who knows how to ask." Listening informs our questions and ergo determines what we learn, what kind of responses we receive and whether we probe to hear the truth or not. Listening shapes our vocabulary. Listening can offer food for thought or simply confirm what we already think we know. We can listen with a bias toward preserving the past or leading the way to the future. Listening facilitates cohesiveness. It is a tool of alignment. Author and professor Otto Scharmer surmises, "Leadership in this century means shifting the structure of collective attention—our listening—at all levels" [32].

Beyond the words we choose, how we say them is equally important. Language can enroll or repel. I call this the *Speak to be Heard* factor. We tend to shut down when people yell at us or when they seem unnaturally monotone or terse. How we say things determines the psychological safety of the interaction. Everything said, or not said, delivers a message, which makes mastering language a priority for leaders. Author Jim Collins reminds us, "Leadership is equally about creating a climate where truth is heard and the brutal facts confronted. There's a huge difference between the opportunity to 'have your say' and the opportunity to be heard" [71]. Speaking to be heard and creating an environment where others can be heard is what Aesthetically Intelligent leaders do.

Though leaders are selected based on their potential or past performance, they are ultimately evaluated by what is unknown—what the journey will be, not what it was or is. I am writing this book during one of the most amazing political years. Politics aside, it is fact that President Barack Obama's journey will become an interdisciplinary source of study for decades to come. During the second Presidential debate, Barack Obama responded to one interrogation by saying something like, "A President must bring the leadership skills to confront what will be, the unknown and even unpredictable events of the future." This statement resonated with me. Think about it. We rise as leaders based on historical and current achievements. But leadership is judged in hindsight following performance in situations that were unknown at the time of selection or election. This is as true for presidents as it is for any of the business leaders mentioned in this book. These examples serve up questions on leadership, your leadership. *What makes you prepared to lead for what is unknown? What skills would that require? Who do you know, personally or professionally, who demonstrates such capability?* I suggest that when you answer these questions, you will see that leaders for the future are present. They are absorbing the entire landscape in real time, integrating, and synthesizing. They preempt and/or diffuse crisis, and they make history in the moment by staying in character and being believable with the various constituencies they serve—by being authentic.

Great leadership is about a way of being, not a segregated list of competencies and techniques. Leadership is a dance of feeling, thought, and expression that guides decisions and behavior. In the text *Leadership is an Art*, Max DePree, Chairman of Herman Miller, summarizes, "The first responsibility of a leader is to define reality. The last is to say thank you. In between the two, the leader must become a servant and a debtor. That sums up the progress of an artful leader" [72]. Great leaders are onstage, performing in front of and with thousands of employees, customers, and other stakeholders, while choreographing the course of an organization's future.

Leadership then is defined by human interactions, engaging hearts and minds, inspiring, igniting, and aligning individual intrinsic motivation with the collective organization. Leaders do not control but rather set the tone and lead by example. Great leaders know who they are. They are innovative and transcend limits. I suggest the elements of AeI©, presence, authenticity and synthesis, equip and strengthen one with the capacity to lead.

In our final section, we will explore how and why an Aesthetically Intelligent leader and an Aesthetically Intelligent culture is better prepared to flourish in times of relentless change and opportunity and are able to move with certainty in uncertain environments.

WHAT WILL YOU DO DIFFERENTLY IN YOUR SPHERE OF INFLUENCE?

The Language of Leadership

- ❏ Complete the Aesthetic Intelligence Self-Assessment in the appendix. Forward your responses to me at rochelle@businessasperformanceart.com and I will e-mail you a completed form with desired responses. Use this to identify key areas of self-development. This assessment can also be adapted and used as a multirater tool with leadership teams and stakeholders. Please contact me for customization.

- ❏ Get your hands dirty. Walk the floor. Ask, "How do employees view their work world?" You can't remove the obstacles to employee engagement from the penthouse floor. Listen, learn, and act. Heed the wisdom of Yogi Berra, "You can observe a lot just by watching."

- ❏ Take personal responsibility. When in a pickle, ask, "What did I do to contribute to this problem?" Ask this often. Look inward before seeking blame outward. When you look in the mirror, see glass, see people, objects, and behavior beyond your singular image.

- ❏ At the end of each day, ask yourself, "What have I done to keep employees engaged?"

- ❏ Pay attention to your choice of words. Calling someone a subordinate may be commonplace but can also be demeaning. Embracing a "sub" mindset of places you higher than others. Think and say "coworkers" and/or "direct reports" in lieu of "subordinates," and you move from order-giver to collaborator. Change a mindset, and you change the dynamics. Change a mindset, and you can redefine a culture and relationships.

- [ ] Become an outrageous inner coach. When those nasty, debilitating inner critic voices pop up in your head, talk back. Be your own best friend. Speak to yourself in the ways you would counsel your best friend. Heed that advice and squash the inner critic. Absent positive self-talk, those inner voices can prove to be your worst enemy.

- [ ] Complete the Emotional Recall activity introduced earlier in the "Artistic Mindset" chapter. *Who are the actors in your life story and how do they make you feel? How can you tap on that experience today? Are you a "when" or a "what" leader?*

- [ ] Reflect on your presence. Do you act on assumptions or truly engage with others? Do you ask a lot of questions, probe for information? Are you giving people your full attention or multitasking? Work on engaging with others to enhance your focus and presence.

- [ ] Say the alphabet backwards. The first time, it takes a lot of concentration and visual recall. Keep practicing and you will notice how much easier it gets, and eventually it will feel as mindless as saying the alphabet forward. This is a neat way to viscerally distinguish between being present and not.

- [ ] List the reasons why you are a leader prepared to lead for what is unknown, the events that are yet to happen but cannot be predicted. Reflect on your career to date that justifies your list. Identify leaders you know who demonstrate such capability. Create a plan to strengthen your presence for these unknown future events.

- [ ] Check out the **L** words. *What are you doing well? Not well? Not at all?* Remedy the situation.

- Inventory your strengths and those of your team. *Are you building strengths or wasting time trying to make weaknesses mediocre?* Surround yourself with complementary talents and delegate tasks that are not your strength.

- Know thyself. Think before you act. Be conscious of your actions and choices. The better we understand ourselves, the more likely we can remain in the moment, and the better our relationships will be.

- Take note of how often you are surprised. If you are not surprised often, then it is likely you are not in the moment or employing generative conversation. You will know when you are enhancing your interactions when you and others walk away surprised with new knowledge and alternative points of view.

- Reframe! When life deals you a lemon, make lemonade. *What do you perceive as your greatest liability?* Pivot that perception into a strength. The ability to reframe thoughts about a problem or situation, to remove an old mental frame and replace it with a new one, is to discover how to strengthen a situation rather than become a victim of it.

- Reframe feedback, as a *valentine*, a gift of information you share and hear, that helps to align intentions and outcomes. Without this information, no one can expect you to change, and you should not expect anyone else to change. Without feedback, assumptions become fact that often taint and weaken relationships. Seek out and give *valentines* to those with whom you work and care about.

- Dare to share. If you are keeping back information for fear of looking stupid, rethink that flawed logic. The more you share, the more likely someone else will give you the information you need.

- ❏ Play off others in group meetings. Practice, "Yes, And." Build on their leads. Make everyone look brilliant.

- ❏ Ask folks around you and beyond, "Is it safe to bring bad news to leadership?" and take appropriate action as needed. Leaders must show that speaking up is not just safe but expected and rewarded.

- ❏ Practice your probing skills by interviewing people to gain an understanding of how folks arrive at their decision-making. The decision could be about a vacation, job, piece of furniture, marriage, etc. The decision is less important than your effort to surface the tacit as well as the known reasons for the choice.

- ❏ Experiment with thinking backwards. Identify an outcome, decision, or action (purchase of new equipment, reorganizing a department, establishing or eliminating a role, pricing, etc.) and work backwards to get to the root of the thinking behind it. Thinking about thinking is not easy, but it proves to be a first step in broadening and changing how you think.

- ❏ Analyze a conversation that did not go as expected, that ended with a clear clash of positions. Drawing on the work of Peter Senge and Chris Argyris, explain the objective of the failed interaction in one paragraph. In the next paragraph, state what your intention was and what you hoped would have happened. Then, to the best of your ability, recall the actual conversation. Create two columns, and in the right column, record the actual words and flow. When finished, revisit the right column, and this time, record on the left side what you think happened that caused the conversation to go the way it did. In the final paragraph, pull it all together, and reflect on how your actions or words (beliefs, assumptions, judgments, and selectivity) contributed to the disappointing outcome. Ask yourself what you could have done differently and what you have learned and will do differently in the future.

- ❏ Create five line portraits to facilitate self-knowledge. Daniel Pink suggests this brief activity as an icebreaker. For example, at the beginning of a meeting, each participant would be asked to draw a self-portrait, using only five continuous lines to express how he or she is feeling at that moment. The lines can be straight or curved. A quick sharing can be enlightening or humorous and serve to set the stage for the meeting. However, this activity can also be used to foster reflection. Getting a visceral response—annoyed, nervous, delighted … draw it with five lines. Ask yourself, "What's going on? What can I learn from this activity?"

- ❏ Reflect on your favorite fairy tale or fictional character growing up. Are there similarities between you and that story's principle character or your favorite heroine or hero? How do these similarities show up to either expand or limit your perceptions and behavior?

- ❏ Tell stories. Good conversation and storytelling satisfies a primal need. A flashy and streamlined PowerPoint presentation does not. Connect the dots of your stories with segues. Rehearse!

- ❏ Borrow methods from grade school and use pictures instead of words to explore and present ideas.

What additional ideas would you add to this list?

DRAMATURGY OF CHANGE

A long habit of not thinking a thing wrong gives it a superficial appearance of being right.
Thomas Paine

One of the ensemble companies I worked with during my dissertation research was producing the play *Brooklyn Boy* and afforded me a unique, one-time experience of serving as a dramaturg. The play is set in Brooklyn, my birthplace and home for my first twenty-six years. It is the story of a writer, Eric Weiss, who at last achieves success with a quasi-autobiographical novel. He escapes from Brooklyn to Hollywood, only to find himself confronted with his childhood demons upon his return to Brooklyn to see his dying, forever disapproving, father. On one hand, the play is a drama of self-discovery that transcends age, gender, and religion. On the other hand, it is a comedy about Brooklyn, and more specifically about Brooklyn Jews, their rituals, language, and other ethnicities. The hospital scenes take place in Maimonides Hospital, where my son was born and my mother died.

This is why I got to switch hats from observer to dramaturg. The director was not Jewish, and there were several times during rehearsal that questions about Jewish traditions and behavior came up for discussion. As a Jewish girl from Brooklyn, I had firsthand experience to offer. That is what a dramaturg does; he or she offers insight to help interpret the screenwriter's intention and keep the production honest. The dramaturg can bring real-time experience as I did or conduct research to ensure accurate depictions of characters, language, locations, customs, social conditions, time periods, and other aspects of the production. The work of the dramaturg is called dramaturgy and is independent of the ensemble's creative activities. It is a design role, one that ensures credibility, fluidity. The dramaturg serves as a guardian and spokesperson for the absent playwright.

So what does this snippet on my dramaturg experience have to do with AeI© and change? As I neared the end of writing this book, I realized I would be remiss not to connect the dots between my extensive experience with individual and organizational change and AeI©. In this way, I offer myself as your dramaturg, and in keeping with the objective of dramaturgy, I intend to share some truths and perspectives on the vast and always important topic of change. I trust you will come to see how the elements of AeI©, presence, authenticity and synthesis, and the medium of AeI©, generative conversation, position individuals and organizations to be more agile and responsive in times of planned and unplanned change.

Truth One: *Change is not new or unique to any generation.*

In the 1990s I worked with a few then Big 6 firms. I was part of the change management practice that supported their bustling management consulting business. Phrases like "Change or Die" or "Survival is not Compulsory" were common. Management guru and author Marvin Weisbord described the rate of change then as being "more like a bullet train than a melting iceberg." [73]. Twenty years later, Generations X and Y are clamoring a similar mantra that change is relentless. No doubt, Generation Z will continue the notion that change is unique to its time. It is not. We are not special.

The truth is that change is a constant. Sometimes it is welcomed; sometimes it is not. Sometimes it is expected; sometimes it is a surprise. What varies with change is not its existence but rather its velocity—whether the change is optional or mandated and how much disruption it creates. Today, instant access and exposure through technology make change ferocious, and these changes leave us panting just trying to keep up. Products and services appear to be outdated before they are even worn-out—quick to market and even quicker to lose their intended competitive advantage.

Truth Two: *Change makes you stupid.*

Change always results in doing or knowing something differently than we did before. Therefore, by definition, change is inseparable from the learning process. As Dilbert says, "Change makes you stupid!" The moment something new presents itself, we become incompetent. Movement confirms our imperfection. Whether that new thing is the awkward use of equipment, the lost feeling of relocation, or the awkwardness you feel when you can't mindlessly reach for toilet paper while staying in a hotel, change makes us stupid.

Truth Three: *Change is both a noun and a verb.*

As a noun, change refers to the outcome, the desired state or objective, which is being pursued such as replacing manual work by implementing enterprise wide software, restructuring the organizational chart and responsibilities, a merger or acquisition, new office space and/or equipment, and more. As a verb, change refers to movement, getting from where you are to where you want to be. The *verb* change is the time of transition.

The perils of change reside in the transition, the movement from the beginning to the desired place. Change in and of itself is not the challenge; it is the transition, the getting there, the movement that is disruptive and must be predicted and planned for. Whether the change is welcomed (a promotion, new home, marriage) or unwelcomed (layoff, divorce, illness), change is always disruptive. Let me say that again. Change is *always* disruptive. The only variable is how disruptive. It is the magnitude and scope of real and/or perceived disruption that dictates the range and depth of actions that individuals and organizations must make. One size does not fit all! Welcomed or not, both types of change require preparation. The transition is plagued with disruption; hence, it is the *verb* change that is problematic, not the *noun*.

Truth Four: *Change is about legitimate concerns, not resistance.*

I have a real problem with the label "resistance." Imagine if we were together right now in a work session and I stormed over to you, pointed my finger, and shouted, "You are resistant!" What would you feel? This is not a trick question. You would feel defensive and rightfully so. This is a classic example of the power of language and how it shapes relationships and defines the dialogue. Let's review an alternative scenario.

What if with a change on the horizon, leaders reached out to stakeholders impacted by the change and asked them to identify their worries, the sources of their "resistance." Likely, they would accumulate a worry list similar to this one:

- Loss of individual control as the future replaces the comfortable past.

- Fear of being able to do the new work.

- Fatigue and time management challenges from working the old and the new processes side by side.

- Loss of future pictures as assumed career opportunities vanish with new requirements.

- Confusion about reporting relationships and accountability.

- Frustration heightened because of lack of information and involvement.

- Worry about job security, income, and life responsibilities.

I suggest this is a list of what I call *legitimate concerns* (See Figure 7.), not resistance, and that if leaders of change reframed their mindset in this manner, their language and approach would dramatically change as well. Empathy and a posture of inquiry would replace impatient accusations of resistance; lack of cooperation and consequently rumor, misinformation, political behavior and disengagement would be replaced with healthy compliance. Reframing enables leaders to honor the past as they confront the paradox of the old and the new, utilizing the language of collaboration, not coercion.

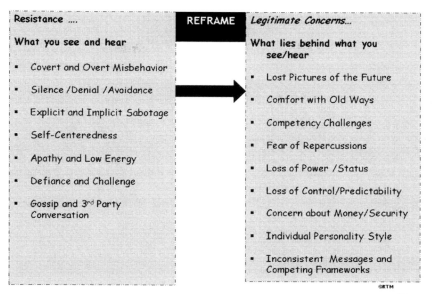

Figure 7

Truth Five: *Leadership's job is to predict and prepare for change.*

The fundamental job of leadership is to deal with the dynamics of change, large and small, short- and long-term, and the multitude of disruptions and transitions that accompany change. Great companies and leaders will not be distinguished by their ability to respond to change quickly and appropriately; they will be distinguished by their ability to respond quickly and deliver with the best rapid response.

In sum, we can see that change disrupts habits, patterns, and expectations. It creates ambiguity about our roles, competencies, responsibilities, status, relationships, compensation, self, and other aspects of our fate. Disruption lessens our ability to control our environment and forces us to operate outside our individual comfort zone. Thus, the goal of change management is to minimize disruption in order to optimize implementation and return on investment. Although the work of change management is not about changing organizational culture, the culture will evolve appropriately as the nature of how work is done changes.

Navigating change demands the acknowledgement that transition is a psychological process that everyone goes through on the journey to accepting a new situation. Leaders of change facilitate fluid information sharing, keep people informed, break down obstacles between people and process, connect the dots, recognize that everyone needs to be involved, know what is driving the need for change, and understand what they and others are contributing to the organization. Leaders listen and address people's legitimate concerns and do not discount it as resistance. They confront failure as learning opportunities without losing the faith or the confidence of their constituency. Leaders demonstrate patience and send a clear message that persistence over time is preferred to quick fixes. They engage stakeholders at every level, mobilize energy and model the confidence to face the unknown without answers. They lead members from the present, through transition to the desired state—through denial, confusion and renewal. They know that commitment cannot be commanded; it must be volunteered. Research documents show that the absence of these actions and behavior accounts for the largest reasons why change initiatives fall short of their objectives.

If we list out what leaders of change need to do, it becomes evident how AeI© strengthens our individual and collective arsenal to move through the change process. (See Figure 8.)

Change leaders seek to maintain harmony, accept endings and beginnings, create a future while honoring the past, simultaneously act and think, and know they are on a journey of continual cyclical change. Cultivating AeI© ensures the agile acts and attitudes required to predict, plan for, and move through ongoing change with the least amount of disruption and the maximum results. This is the power and potential of AeI©, to be present, intentionally authentic, quick to synthesis and choose the language of generative conversation.

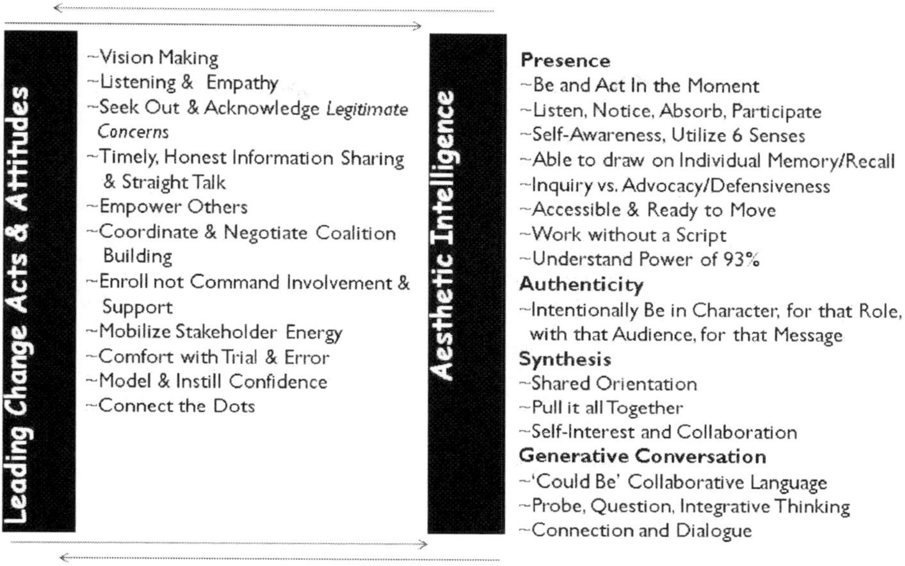

DRAMATURGY OF CHANGE 153

Leading Change Acts & Attitudes
- Vision Making
- Listening & Empathy
- Seek Out & Acknowledge *Legitimate Concerns*
- Timely, Honest Information Sharing & Straight Talk
- Empower Others
- Coordinate & Negotiate Coalition Building
- Enroll not Command Involvement & Support
- Mobilize Stakeholder Energy
- Comfort with Trial & Error
- Model & Instill Confidence
- Connect the Dots

Aesthetic Intelligence

Presence
- Be and Act In the Moment
- Listen, Notice, Absorb, Participate
- Self-Awareness, Utilize 6 Senses
- Able to draw on Individual Memory/Recall
- Inquiry vs. Advocacy/Defensiveness
- Accessible & Ready to Move
- Work without a Script
- Understand Power of 93%

Authenticity
- Intentionally Be in Character, for that Role, with that Audience, for that Message

Synthesis
- Shared Orientation
- Pull it all Together
- Self-Interest and Collaboration

Generative Conversation
- 'Could Be' Collaborative Language
- Probe, Question, Integrative Thinking
- Connection and Dialogue

Figure 8

WHAT WILL YOU DO DIFFERENTLY IN YOUR SPHERE OF INFLUENCE?

Dramaturgy of Change

Instead of a list of possible actions, I am going to share my Change Management approach. When working with big consulting firms, I was dumbfounded by how complex they made the process of managing change, and I felt compelled to create something much simpler, more flexible, and much easier to talk about. (See Figure 9.)

The notion that Change Management work is not limited to a phase or step but rather interdependent with all other tasks and ongoing throughout the life of a given initiative govern my approach. Specific activities are determined based on the initiative scope, magnitude, and impact of change and disruption for the client organization. AeI© capacity is woven throughout.

Change Management begins at the onset of the initiative with an assessment to ensure a shared understanding of the current client environment. Information is gathered through informal and formal methods to gain a snapshot of how the organization and its members work together. Assessment data identifies leverages that will help, as well as misalignments that will hinder implementing the desired change. Potential actions and priorities are explored. These results inform and prioritize Change Management planning. Additional activities during this time include working with sponsorship to clarify expectations and responsibilities, selecting internal resources, and educating and developing the work teams.

Alignment activities seek to build stakeholder understanding and support of the project—that is, prepare the membership for implementation and correct misalignments that would compromise the success of business goals.

Connection strategy ensures that all impacted individuals and groups are informed, hear clear and consistent messages, share a common language, and understand the process, expectations, and predicted outcomes. Connection is not public relations. Connection and conversation take on many forms and mediums to foster trust, diminish ambiguity, and lessen occurrences of rumors and misinformation.

Education prepares all members for their roles and responsibilities by teaching the knowledge, skills, and behaviors required to design, conduct, implement, and sustain desired results.

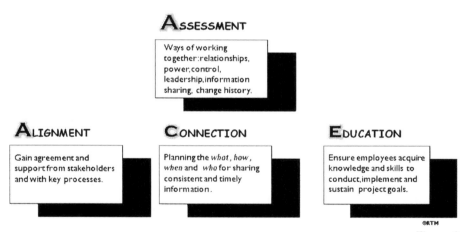

Figure 9

How does this resonate with your "change approach?" How might this approach influence how you predict and plan for change?

NOT THE CLOSING CURTAIN

There are risks and costs to a program of action - but they are far less than the long-range risks and costs of comfortable inaction.
John F. Kennedy

We began our journey by exploring the culture of the performing arts as a first step toward appreciating how its culture embodies the coveted attributes most business organizations crave. The underpinning of this enviable culture is Aesthetic Intelligence, a capacity that embraces the full utility and power of our senses, defined by Presence, Authenticity, and Synthesis, and makes itself evident through Generative Conversation.

We visited companies that showed us that when Aesthetic Intelligence is translated into systems and processes, it cultivates a culture of connection, creativity, and innovation fueled by engaged and collaborative employees and steered by masterful leadership. These interdependent elements come together and enable organizations to create and sustain successful performance in an ever changing, diverse and global marketplace.

Aesthetically Intelligent leaders have more questions than answers and know there is more than one good answer. They accept their incompleteness and not only remain in search of the next incremental possibility but also want to be a part of the action that unveils it. They welcome the emergent and advocate evolution, not revolution. They recognize the danger of not evolving. Aesthetic Intelligence offers a palette of opportunities to reconceive our roles and organizations.

I hope I have achieved my stated objectives.

- *Did I provoke your curiosity? Spark ideas? Trigger an aha? Illuminate a connection? Offer a surprise?*
- *Did you discover a golden nugget? Can you imagine possibilities?*

I hope I have begun a conversation.

- *Will you continue the exploration?*
- *Are you opting to be Davy Crockett or a wagon follower?*

It is likely that when you began this book, you were not familiar with Aesthetic Intelligence and much of the content. You were from a learning perspective, *unconsciously incompetent*—that is, you did not know what you did not know. (See Figure 10.) If you resonate with the content, then you moved up a step, and now may feel *consciously incompetent*—you know what you do not know. Experimenting with new ways of thinking and doing will land you on the *consciously competent* step where actions are deliberate, take more time, and often feel awkward. With practice, repetition, and discipline, you will arrive at being *unconsciously competent*—mindful but no longer awkward. Mastery of anything does not happen by accident. It happens with choice, by seeking out the experiences you need and allowing ample the time to learn and grow.

Aesthetic Intelligence is a human capacity that is beyond the limits of any specific industry, role, era, generation, demographic, or trend. We are born with this innate capacity. I hope you will choose to reclaim the power of your senses and develop your Aesthetic Intelligence.

When we look at what we do in business as performance art and we cultivate an artistic mindset, we spark new ways of thinking about living and work. The intersection and collaboration of these diverse fields extends the breadth of their individual and collective contributions. There is much to learn and I believe we have only just begun. I welcome you on this journey.

Performance is a work in progress!

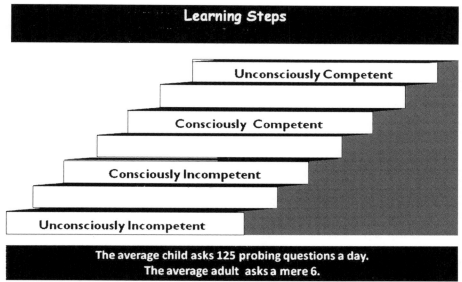

Figure 10

APPENDIX ONE

Ael© Self-Assessment

The following pages present forty phrases describing specific behaviors and activities.

Please read each carefully; then rate yourself in terms of how frequently you believe you engage in the practice described. Record your response by drawing a circle around the number that corresponds to the frequency you have selected. There are no right or wrong answers. You are given six choices:

1. If you *rarely or very seldom* do what is described in the statement, circle, "1."
2. If you do what is described *once in a while,* circle "2."
3. If you *sometimes* do what is described, circle "3."
4. If you do what is described *fairly often,* circle "4."
5. If you do what is described *very frequently or almost always,* circle "5."
6. If you are uncertain of what the question is asking, or *unsure* of how to respond, circle "6."

In selecting the answer, be realistic about the extent to which you actually engage in each behavior. Do not answer in terms of how you would like to see yourself behave or in terms of what you *should* be doing. Answer in terms of how you *typically behave.* There is additional space provided for comments. This is optional. Please use this section to provide any additional examples or situations that support your response.

To what extent do I engage in the following actions and behaviors? Circle the number that applies to each statement.

1	2	3	4	5	6
Rarely or very seldom	Once in awhile	Sometimes	Fairly often	Very frequently or almost always	Unsure

1. I play to my strengths.
       1   2   3   4   5   6

Comments:

2. I am passionate about my work.
       1   2   3   4   5   6

Comments:

3. I am available to new ideas.
       1   2   3   4   5   6

Comments:

4. Conversations rarely surprise me.
       1   2   3   4   5   6

Comments:

5. I approach people and projects with an attitude of what "should be" vs. what "could be."
       1   2   3   4   5   6

Comments:

6. I often leave interactions with renewed energy.
       1   2   3   4   5   6

Comments:

7. When I enter a given setting, I make note of people, objects, and movement.
       1   2   3   4   5   6

Comments:

8. My behavior and rhetoric demonstrates that self-interest and collaboration are interdependent.

           1   2   3   4   5   6

Comments:

9. I am impatient with process.

           1   2   3   4   5   6

Comments:

10. People I meet with leave our interaction with renewed energy.

           1   2   3   4   5   6

Comments:

To what extent do I engage in the following actions and behaviors? Circle the number that applies to each statement.

1	2	3	4	5	6
Rarely or very seldom	Once in awhile	Sometimes	Fairly often	Very frequently or almost always	Unsure

11. I reflect on my interactions and decisions on a daily basis.

        1   2   3   4   5   6

Comments:

12. I avoid providing timely and direct feedback to others.

        1   2   3   4   5   6

Comments:

13. I ask for feedback on a daily basis.

        1   2   3   4   5   6

Comments:

14. I approach conflict in a timely, direct, and healthy manner.

        1   2   3   4   5   6

Comments:

15. Before interactions, I consider how best to achieve my objectives (facilitate, report, influence, advise, respond, etc.) with the specific audience and context.

        1   2   3   4   5   6

Comments:

16. People I work with are content with their role and contribution.

        1   2   3   4   5   6

Comments:

17. My decision making process is transparent.

        1   2   3   4   5   6

Comments:

APPENDIX ONE 165

18. I am known for being an 'idea stopper' (won't work here, not in the budget) rather than an 'idea starter' (tell me more, what if).

                1   2   3   4   5   6

Comments:

19. I model learning from, rather than, punishing mistakes.

                1   2   3   4   5   6

Comments:

20. I tolerate, as opposed to appreciate, accept, and respect, different work styles.

                1   2   3   4   5   6

Comments:

To what extent do I engage in the following actions and behaviors? Circle the number that applies to each statement.

1	2	3	4	5	6
Rarely or very seldom	Once in awhile	Sometimes	Fairly often	Very frequently or almost always	Unsure

21. I consciously balance observation and reflection.
               1   2   3   4   5   6

Comments:

22. I have difficulty shifting my point of view in real time.
               1   2   3   4   5   6

Comments:

23. I am easily distracted during conversations and meetings.
               1   2   3   4   5   6

Comments:

24. I am bothered by fluctuation and/or surprise at work.
               1   2   3   4   5   6

Comments:

25. I dread hearing bad news from others.
               1   2   3   4   5   6

Comments:

26. I feel truthful.
               1   2   3   4   5   6

Comments:

27. I am accessible to listen to people's concerns.
               1   2   3   4   5   6

Comments:

28. My daily actions feel routine.
               1   2   3   4   5   6

Comments:

29. I am not conscious of why I sit or position myself in a room full of others.

                      1   2   3   4   5   6

Comments:

30. I relish the "aha" of seeing underlying patterns emerge.

                      1   2   3   4   5   6

Comments:

To what extent do I engage in the following actions and behaviors? Circle the number that applies to each statement.

1	2	3	4	5	6
Rarely or very seldom	Once in awhile	Sometimes	Fairly often	Very frequently or almost always	Unsure

31. I am aware of the influence my sensory experiences have on my behavior and decision-making.
        1   2   3   4   5   6
Comments:

32. I am clear about my intentions for any given interaction.
        1   2   3   4   5   6
Comments:

33. I fester after meetings or conversations, rather than voicing my thoughts in real time.
        1   2   3   4   5   6
Comments:

34. I consistently probe to see the world through other people's eyes.
        1   2   3   4   5   6
Comments:

35. I demonstrate the coexistence of structure and freedom.
        1   2   3   4   5   6
Comments:

36. I embrace a sense of play at work.
        1   2   3   4   5   6
Comments:

37. I distinguish between 'being' and 'doing'.
        1   2   3   4   5   6
Comments:

38. I predict events or actions before they happen.
          1   2   3   4   5   6
Comments:

39. I feel comfortable with who I am and how I perform in most situations.
          1   2   3   4   5   6
Comments:

40. I feel optimistic.
          1   2   3   4   5   6
Comments:

Please transfer your ratings below.

1. _____
2. _____
3. _____
4. _____
5. _____
6. _____
7. _____
8. _____
9. _____
10. _____
11. _____
12. _____
13. _____
14. _____
15. _____
16. _____
17. _____
18. _____
19. _____
20. _____
21. _____
22. _____
23. _____
24. _____
25. _____
26. _____
27. _____
28. _____
29. _____
30. _____
31. _____
32. _____

33. _____
34. _____
35. _____
36. _____
37. _____
38. _____
39. _____
40. _____

APPENDIX TWO

List of Interviewees

Alliance Theatre
  Actor, *David*
  Actor, *Chris*
  Actor, *Joe*
  Actor, *Neal*
  Understudy Actor, *David S.*
  Director, *BJ*
  Stage Manager, *Kate*

Jewish Theatre of the South
  Actor, *Isaac*
  Actor, *Bruce*
  Actor, *Renee*
  Actor, *Maggie*
  Director, *Sarah*
  Producer, *Susan*
  Production/Stage Manager, *Blake*
  Technical Director, *Bob*
  Lighting Designer, *Chris*

APPENDIX THREE

Recommended Resources

Adler, N., *The Art of Leadership: Now That We Can Do Anything, What Do We Want To Do?* Academy of Management Education & Learning Journal, 2006. 5(4): p. 466–499.

Austin, R., & Devin, L. (2003). *Artful making: what managers need to know.* Upper Saddle River Prentice Hall.

Brown, T., *Design Thinking.* Harvard Business Review, 2008. June.

Catmull, E., *How Pixar Fosters Collective Creativity.* Harvard Business Review, 2008(September).

Clark, T., & Mangham, I. (2004). From dramaturgy to theatre as technology: the case of corporate theatre. *Journal of Management Studies, 41*(1), 37–59.

David Whyte's (1994) *The Heart Aroused: Poetry and the Preservation of the Soul in Corporate America.* New York: Currency Doubleday.

Davis, S., & McIntosh, D. (2005). *The Art of Business: Making All Your Work A Work of Art.* San Francisco: Berrett-Koehler.

DePree, M. (1989). *Leadership is an art.* New York Doubleday.

DePree, M. (1992). *Leadership jazz.* New York Dell.

Drucker, P., *Managing Oneself.* Harvard Business Review, 1999.

Florida, Richard (2002) *The Rise of the Creative Class.* New York: Basic Books.

Gilmore, J., & Pine, J. (2007). *Authenticity.* Boston: Harvard Business School Press.

Goffman, E. (1959). *The presentation of self in everyday life.* New York Anchor.

Guber, P., *The four truths of the storyteller.* Harvard Business Review, 2007: p. 52–62.

Ibbotson, P., *The Illusion of Leadership.* 2008, Palgrave, London.

Johnstone, K., *Impro.* 1987, New York: Routledge.

Kao, J.J. (1996) *The Art and Discipline of Business Creativity.* New York: Harper Business.

Kegan, R. and L. Lahey, *How the way we talk can change the way we work.* 2001, San Francisco: Jossey-Bass.

Langer, E.J., *Mindfulness.* 1989, Menlo Park California: Addison-Wesley Publishing Company, Inc.

March, J., & Coutu, D. (2006). Ideas as art. *Harvard Business Review*(October), 82–89.

Mintzberg, H., The manager's job: folklore and fact. Harvard Business Review, 1990(March-April).

Mirvis, P., *Executive Development through Consciousness-Raising Experiences.* Academy of Management Education & Learning Journal, 2008. 7(2): p. 173.

Morgan, G. (1993). *Imaginization: the art of creative management.* California: Sage.

Mucha, R. (2005). Business as performance art. *Organization Development Journal, 23*(3).

Mucha, R. (2007). *Business as Performance Art: Exploring the Relationship between People, Passion, and Performance.* Dissertation, Fielding Graduate University, Santa Barbara.

Mucha, R. (2007). Insights from Theatre on Talent and Alignment, ODN Seasonings, Volume 4, Number1, Winter 2008.

Mucha, R., *Aesthetic Intelligence: Cultivating an Artistic Mindset.* Organization Development Journal, 2008 (Fall).

Pine, B. J., & Gilmore, J. H. (1999). *The experience economy.* Boston Harvard Business School Press

Pink, Daniel H. (2005) *A Whole New Mind: Why Right-Brainers Will Rule theWorld.* New York: Riverhead (Penguin Group).

Postrel, V. (2003). *The Substance of Style: How the Rise of Aesthetic Value is Remaking Culture.* New York: Harper Collins.

Sawyer, K., *Group Genius.* 2007, New York Basic Books.

Schein, E., *Organizational culture and leadership*. 1985, San Francisco: Jossey-Bass Publishers.

Seifter, Harvey (2001) *Leadership Ensemble: Lessons in Collaborative Management from the World's Only Conductorless Orchestra*. New York: Holt/Times Books.

Tharp, Twyla (2003) *The Creative Habit: Learn it and Use it for Life*. New York: Simon & Schuster Paperbacks.

Zander, R. and B. Zander, *The Art of Possibility: Transforming professional and personal life*. 2000, Boston: Harvard Business School Press.

REFERENCES

1. Griffin, V., *Holistic Teaching and Learning: Would You Play A One String Guitar*, in *The Craft of Teaching Adults*. 1993, Culture Concepts: Toronto.
2. Pine, B.J. and J.H. Gilmore, *The experience economy*. 1999, Boston Harvard Business School Press
3. Mucha, R., *Business as Performance Art: Exploring the Relationship between People, Passion, and Performance*, in *Human and Organizational Development*. 2007, Fielding Graduate University: Santa Barbara. p. 350.
4. Mandelbaum, K., *A chorus line and the musicals of Michael Bennett*. 1989, New York St. Martin's Press.
5. Flinn, D.M., *What they did for love*. 1989, New York Bantam Books.
6. Austin, R. and L. Devin, *Artful making: what managers need to know*. 2003, Upper Saddle River Prentice Hall.
7. Alda, A., *Never have your dog stuffed*. 2005, New York: Random House.
8. Schatz, H., *In character: actors acting*. 2006, New York Bullfinch Publishers.
9. Whyte, D., *The Heart Aroused*. 1994, New York: Currency Doubleday.
10. Zander, R. and B. Zander, *The Art of Possibility: Transforming professional and personal life*. 2000, Boston: Harvard Business School Press.
11. Mirvis, P., *Practice Improvisation*. Organization Science, 1998. 9(5): p. 586–594.
12. Tischler, *MOD*, in *Fast Company*. 2007. p. 90–100.

13. Postrel, V., *The Substance of Style: How the Rise of Aesthetic Value is Remaking Culture.* 2003, New York: Harper Collins.
14. Pink, D., *A Whole New Mind.* 2005, New York: Penguin Group.
15. Darso, L., *Artful Creation. Learning-Tales of Arts-in-Business.* 2004, Fredeiriksberg: Samfundslitteratur.
16. Board, T.C., *Ready to Innovate.* 2008, The Conference Board.
17. MBA, U.G., *The Good Times Continue to Roll,* in *Harvard Business Review.* 2008.
18. University, H., *Report of the Task Force on the Arts.* 2008, Harvard University Harvard University.
19. Anders, G., *Business Schools Forgetting Missions?,* in *Wall Street Journal.* 2007: New York. p. A2.
20. Zaleznik, A., *Managers and leaders: are they different?* Harvard Business Review, 1977(May-June).
21. Mucha, R. and C. Goodwin. *Aesthetic Intelligence: What Business Can Learn From The World Of The Arts.* in *Art of Management* 2008. Banff, Canada.
22. Gardner, H., *Frames of mind: The theory of multiple intelligences.* 10th ed. 1983, New York: Basic Books.
23. Goleman, D., *Emotional intelligence* 1995, New York: Bantam Books.
24. Goleman, D. and R. Boyatzis, *Social Intelligence and the biology of leadership.* Harvard Business Review, 2008(September): p. 74-82.
25. Stockil, T. *Ci.* 2007 [cited; Available from: www.creativeintelligence.uk.com.
26. Earley, C. and E. Mosakowski, *Cultural intelligence.* Harvard Business Review, 2004(October): p. 139-149.
27. Zohar, D. and I. Marshall, *SQ:Connecting with our spiritual intelligence.* 2001: Bloomsburg
28. Cohn, J., J. Katzenbach, and G. Vlak, *Finding and grooming breakthrough innovators.* Harvard Business Review, 2008(December): p. 62–72.
29. Senge, P., et al., *Presence.* 2004, New York: Doubleday Broadway.

30. Spencer, M., *It takes two to tango.* Journal of Business Strategy, 2005. 26(5): p. 62–68.
31. Gladwell, M., *Blink.* 2005: Little Brown & Company.
32. Scharmer, C.O., *Theory U.* 2009, California: Berrett-Koehler.
33. Mintzberg, H., *The manager's job: folklore and fact.* Harvard Business Review, 1990(March-April).
34. Hotz, R.L., *Surveying the Brain for Origins of the Senior Moment*, in *Wall Street Journal* 2008: New York p. A14.
35. Johnstone, K., *Impro.* 1987, New York: Routledge.
36. Ackerman, D., *A Natural History of the Senses.* 1990, New York: Vintage.
37. Drucker, P., *Managing Oneself.* Harvard Business Review, 1999.
38. Guber, P., *The four truths of the storyteller.* Harvard Business Review, 2007. December: p. 52–62.
39. Tichy, N. and M.A. Devanna, *The transformational leader.* 1986, New York John Wiley & Sons.
40. Barrett, F., *Creating appreciative learning cultures.* Organizational Dynamics, n.d.: p. 36–49.
41. Florida, R., *The rise of the creative class.* 2002, New York: Basic Books.
42. Conley, L., *Creative confinement*, in *Fast Company.* 2005. p. 99.
43. Martin, R., *The Opposable Mind.* 2007, Boston: Harvard Business School Press
44. Iyer, B. and T. Davenport, *Reverse engineering Google's innovation machine.* Harvard Business Review, 2008(April): p. 59–68.
45. Adler, N., *I Am My Mother's Daughter.* European International Management, 2008. **2**(1): p. 6–21.
46. Kouzes, J. and B. Posner, *Credibility.* 1993, San Francisco: Jossey-Bass.
47. Mirvis, P., *Executive Development through Consciousness-Raising Experiences.* Academy of Management Education & Learning Journal, 2008. **7**(2): p. 173.
48. George, B., et al., *Discovering your authentic leadership.* Harvard Business Review, 2007.

49. *Mergers and Acquisition.* Retrieved in 2006 [cited; Available from: http://executiveeducation.wharton.upenn.edu/course.cfm?Program=MA.
50. Kaplan, R.S. and D.P. Norton, *Alignment.* 2006, Massachusetts: Harvard Business School Press.
51. Drehle, D.V., *Why history can't wait,* in *Time.* 2008.
52. Collins, J. and J. Porras, *Built to last.* 1994, New York: Harper Business.
53. Pfeiffer, J., *No Excuses Leadership.* Leader to Leader, 2007. 46(Fall): p. 31–35.
54. Breen, B., *The 6 myths of creativity.* Fast Company, 2004(December): p. 75–79.
55. Schein, E., *Organizational culture and leadership.* 1985, San Francisco: Jossey-Bass Publishers.
56. Johansson, F., *The Medici Effect: Breakthrough Insights at the Intersection of Ideas.* 2004, Boston: Harvard School Business Press.
57. Catmull, E., *How Pixar Fosters Collective Creativity.* Harvard Business Review, 2008(September).
58. Sawyer, K., *Group Genius.* 2007, New York Basic Books.
59. Tischler, L., *A Designer.* Fast Company, 2009(February).
60. Brown, T., *Design Thinking.* Harvard Business Review, 2008. June.
61. McGirt, E., *Revolution in San Jose.* Fast Company, 2008.
62. Prokesch, S., *How GE Teaches Teams to Lead Change.* Harvard Business Review, 2009(January): p. 99–106.
63. Safian, R., *Fast Company Top 50,* in *Fast Company.* 2009.
64. Mucha, R., *The art and science of talent management* Organization Development Journal, 2004(Winter): p. 96–100.
65. Rutledge, T., *Getting Engaged: The New Workplace Loyalty.* 2006, Canada: Matlanie.
66. Krueger, J. and E. Killham, *Why Dilbert is right.* Gallup Management Journal, 2006(March).
67. Seijts, G. and D. Crim, *What engages employees the most of, the ten c's of employee engagement.* Ivey Business Journal, 2006(March/April).

68. Bennis, W., *On becoming a leader.* 1989, New York: Addison-Wesley
69. Welch, J., *Winning.* 2005, New York Harper Business.
70. Heifetz, R., *The leader of the future,* in *Fast Company.* 1999. p. 130–135.
71. Collins, J., *Good to great.* 2001, New York: Harper-Collins Publishers.
72. DePree, M., *Leadership is an art.* 1989, New York Doubleday.
73. Weisbord, M., *Toward third-wave managing and consulting.* Organizational Dynamics, 1987: p. 5–24.

INDEX

AACORN 22, 193
AASCB 25
A Chorus Line 10–11, 70, 77, 179
Ackerman, Diane 39
Actors 9, 12, 15–19, 27, 33–35, 38, 54–56, 81–82, 85, 115, 119, 130–137, 142
Adler, Nancy 5, 69, 72
Aesthetic, root of 8
Aesthetic Intelligence 29–53, AeI© Graphic, 31
Aesthetic Intelligence Journey 5
Alda, Alan 13
Alignment (misalignment) 79–87, Costs associated with, 80–83
Alliance Theatre 11, 131
Aria.Salon.Spa.Shoppe 84
Artifacts 91–92
Artists 2, 13, 22, 25, 27, 33–34, 43, 50, 95, 97, 115–116, 134–136
Artistic Mindset 27–32, 51–52, 72, 142, 159
Art of Management Conference 27
Assessment 43, 77, 94, 119, 141, 154, 161

Audience (Client, Customer) 9, 15, 21, 43, 77, 85, 105, 131
Austin, Rob 12, 35
Authenticity 8, 42–48, 51–52, 63, 88, 94, 122, 130, 132, 137, 140, 148, 157
Babson University 26
Bennett, Michael 10
Beliefs 16, 19, 91–93
Behar, Yves 23
Boehm, David 40
Booth, Susan 11, 17, 131
Brown, Tim (IDEO) 100, 136
Buffett, Warren 1, 23
Burstyn, Ellen 18
Business Radio Atlanta 28
Candor (Criticism) 18–20, 61
Casting 63, 76, 97, 105, 118–119, 131–133
Catmull, Ed (Pixar) 95, 99, 136
Chambers, John (Cisco) 101–102, 136
Change 3, 16, 20, 25, 31, 38–39, 42, 45, 49, 63–64, 67–68, 72, 77–78, 81–82, 84, 86, 88, 92–93, 98, 101–102, 107, 111, 124, 147–155, Legitimate Concerns (Resistance)

Graphic, 151, Leaders and Graphic, 152, A.A.C.E. Model, 155
Chattahoochee River 79
Cimino, John 22
Cisco 24, 101–103, 118, 121, 136
Collaboration 3, 10, 12, 14–15, 20, 27, 60–62, 77, 85–86, 96–97, 102–104, 121, 128, 132, 135, 137, 150, 159
Collins, Jim 83, 138
Communication (see Connection) 20, 57, 59–63, 76, 80, 91, 102, 106, 137
Competency 12, 15, 20, 26, 31, 93, 104, 117, 121
Compromise (see Collaboration) 12, 14–16, 104, 131
Conference Board 24
Connection 3, 12, 21, 27, 32, 40, 48, 51, 60–67, 72, 87–88, 93–96, 99, 102, 104–106, 114, 122, 128, 130, 155, 157
Crockett, Davy 1, 158
Creative Leadership Forum 61
Creativity 3, 8, 21–28, 32, 49–51, 60–62, 87, 94–105
Culture 3, 9, 11–28, 45, 50–56, 61, 76, 81, 91–113, Culture Graphic, 104
Delta Airlines 45
Design 23, 26, 61, 76, 82, 98–101
Devin, Lee 12, 32

Director 10, 15, 19, 22, 38, 61, 98, 105, 119, 127–147
Dissertation 1–2, 9, 147
Dramaturgy (Dramaturg) 154
Dreyfuss, Richard 17
Drucker, Peter 40, 73, 138
Emotional Intelligence 30
Emotional Memory 54
Empathy 24, 30, 133–138, 150
Energy 12, 21, 32, 49–51, 57, 76, 82, 94, 113–122
Engagement/Disengagement 28, 82, 86, 113–127 Costs associated with, 116
Ensemble 9–16, 33, 63, 76–77, 81–84, 95–98, 105, 113, 119, 130–132, 147
Experience Economy 8
Experimentation (experiment) 12, 17–18, 50, 85, 95–98, 100, 104, 121
Fast Company 23, 32, 94, 99, 101
Feedback 11, 18–22, 38, 48, 62, 73, 76, 85, 97–98, 102–108, 121–123, 128, 143
Gardner, Howard 29, 70
GE (General Electric) 102–105
Generative Conversation 28, 57–67, 157, Power of the 93%, 60, Should Be/Could Be, 64–65, Phrases Graphic, 65
Gilmore, James 8, 44

INDEX

Gladwell, Malcolm (Blink) 34
Global Environment 21, 27, 60, 81, 87, 101–102, 122
Goleman, Daniel 30
Goodwin, Constance 27, 54
Google 61–62
Griffin, Virginia 8
Guber, Peter 45
'Happy Factor' 115
Harvard Business Review 24, 32, 74
Harvard University 22–25
Heifetz, Ronald 22, 138
Hewlett-Packard 24
Hirsch, Mira 11, 81, 131
IDEO 26, 92, 99–102, 118, 136
Imagination 4, 7, 22–25, 35, 51, 60, 76, 93, 103, 105, 115
Improvisation (Improv) also see *Yes, And* 22–26, 34–35, 95, 100, 108
Innovation 3, 21–22, 27–28, 50–51, 60–62, 87–99, 105–106, 130, 157
Intel 24, 63, 136
Intelligence Evolution (IQ, Emotional, Spiritual, Social, Cultural, Creative) 29–31
Intersection of Business and the Arts 2, 23–25, 130
Jazz Ensemble and Collaboration 22–26, 33, 84, 96
Jewish Theatre of the South 11

Johnson & Johnson 23
Kaplan, David 81
Kelley, David 26, 99
Knowledge Age 7
Language (see Generative Conversation)
Leadership (Leader) 22–25, 30, 40, 47, 56, 60–61, 69, 73–76, 83, 89–92, 102–103, 127–147
Learning Graphic, 159
Listening (see Generative Conversation)
Lutz, Robert 23
Martin, Roger (Opposable Mind) 59–60, 64, 103
MBA 24–26, 54, 88
Mental Models (mindlessness) 40, 49
Merger (acquisition) 20, 80, 96, 149
Mintzberg, Henry 34–35
Mission (Purpose) 12, 17, 45–46, 76–84, 92, 100, 106–107
Musician, music 8, 33, 43, 47–49, 65, 117, 131
Nadler, David 77–79
New York University 26
Nike 23
Obama, Barack 40, 63, 136–139
Organizational Aesthetics 2, 22
Passion 9, 12, 22, 24, 70, 76, 81, 85, 89, 95–96, 104, 113–121, 136–137

P & G 24
Perception 8, 49, 73–76, 84, 143–145
Performance 2–3, 9–19, 28, 33, 42–43, 48–52, 57, 65, 76–86, 93–94, 105, 113, 118–122, 131–133, 137, 159
Pfeiffer, Jeffrey 89
Pine, Joseph 8, 44
Pink, Daniel 25, 91, 109
Pioneer 22, 30, 60
Pixar 62, 95–102, 118
Presence 2, 8, 16, 32–42, 48–52, 53, 67, 88, 94, 105, 122, 130, 136, 138, 140, 142, 148, 157
Pride 12, 16, 20–22, 45, 55, 72, 82, 104
Producer 19, 45, 97, 120, 130
Protocol 18–21, 76, 93
Rehearsal 15, 18, 47–49, 63, 85, 97–98, 101, 105, 108, 131–134, 147
Risk (see Experimentation)
SAS 9, 117–118, 136
Sawyer, Keith 6, 100
Scharmer, Otto 34, 138
Schein, Edgar 91
Script 9, 15, 18, 28, 33–35, 40, 43, 61, 69–70, 76, 101, 119, 130, 133
Self-Awareness 30, 40–44, 48–49, 67–74, 116
Self-Interest 12, 15, 85–86, 97, 104

Senge, Peter 41, 74, 144
Senses 7–9, 23–27, 32, 39, 42, 50–52, 72–74, 84, 87–88, 105, 108, 115, 122–124, 157–159
Speak to be Heard Factor 138
Should Be, Could Be Graphic 154
Stanford University, Graduate School of Business 26, 74
Storytelling (also see Guber, Peter) 13, 17, 45, 69, 109, 145
Synthesis 3, 8, 48–53, 59, 63, 88–89, 94, 122, 130–132, 140, 148, 153, 157
Systems Thinking 41, 75, Systems Graphic, 75
Sweet Spot 113–116, 120, 123, Graphic, 114
Talent Management (Recruitment) 20, 76, 118
Technology Age 7, 20, 34–35, 57, 63, 76, 98, 101–106, 117, 148
The Home Depot 80–82
The Medici Effect 93
The Opposable Mind (see Martin, Roger) 59, 103
Tichy, Noel 47, 138
Trust 16, 19, 20, 33, 38–39, 42, 46, 54, 93, 96–98, 101–104, 108, 121, 123, 132, 135, 148, 155

Wharton School of Business 26, 74
Whyte, David 22
W.L. Gore 62, 94–100, 118, 136

Yes, And 35–39, 65, 104, 109, 144
Zaleznik, Abraham 25
Zander, Ben 221
Zappos 119

Rochelle T. Mucha Ph.D. is the founder of Business as Performance Art™, a consulting firm that focuses on strategic leadership, learning, and change. She is a frequent speaker and adjunct business school professor whose articles have appeared in academic and trade journals. As a member of AACORN (Arts, Aesthetics, Creativity and Organization Research Network), she is part of a pioneering group exploring the intersection of Business and the Arts. Prior to forming her consulting business, she served as a Regional Director of Training for Marriott Corporation and was affiliated with several global management consulting firms. Mucha lives in Atlanta, GA and invites readers to contact her at rochelle@businessasperformanceart.com and visit her website at **www.businessasperformanceart.com**

Made in the USA